Hamlyn Colour Guides

Cats

Hamlyn Colour Guides

Cats

by Albert Pintera

Illustrated by Jan Maget

HAMLYN

Text by Albert Pintera
Illustrations by Jan Maget
Translated by Eva Klimentová
Graphic design by František Prokeš
Designed and produced by Artia for
the Hamlyn Publishing Group Limited
a Division of the Octopus Publishing Group plc
Bridge House, London Road,
Twickenham,
Middlesex, England
Printed in Czechoslovakia by Svoboda, Prague
ISBN 0 600 30 6658
3/15/21/51-01

Contents

Introduction

Everyone is familiar with the domestic cat, even if they have never owned one. Who can ignore these enigmatic creatures with their brilliant perceptive eyes, soft coats and inquisitive natures? Although the cat is man's companion, too, just like the dog, it is hardly possible to compare the two. Despite both having a close association with man, and endowed with equal intelligence regarding their ability to communicate with their master, the characters and qualities of these two domestic animals are totally opposite to each other.

It often seems, to people who have not studied the cat's true nature, that cats are aloof and even deceitful animals, and less intelligent than dogs. But what is the truth? In fact, each cat is simply a complete individualist which fends for itself in any situation in life, often seeming to show complete indifference to anything or anybody else. The dog, on the other hand, being a pack animal by nature, is much more dependent on man, whom it sees as a kind of substitute for the pack leader. This dependence has been very well exploited by man. He is aware of the fact that dogs can be more easily dominated and trained than cats, and has used them for a variety of tasks. Therefore the dog usually stands higher in man's esteem than the cat.

The fact that the cat will never be devoted to man in the same way as the dog is probably the reason that it did not become domesticated until much later than the dog. The dog was used initially to guard man's camps and his flocks of animals. When man established more permanent settlements, the cat was seen to be much better equipped at catching vermin, which were now an important concern, particularly where crops and grain were stored.

In Ancient Egypt, as long ago as 2,500 BC, the cat was highly prized and even worshipped. The fertile corn fields in the Nile's river basin were the source of Egypt's power and wealth. Corn was stored in granaries, and the cat helped to protect the crop against mice and rats. In addition, the cat protected the Egyptians from venomous snakes, which were attracted to the granaries in search of food.

Later, the domestic cat's popularity spread to other parts of the world. Although the Ancient Greeks and Romans also revered the cat, surprisingly few depictions of the cat have survived from those times. This was probably the result of religious influences, since the cat was often considered as a goddess in many parts of the world. This was especially true in countries such as Scandinavia, Ireland, China and Peru.

The Christian church was vigorously opposed to the pagan cults. Consequently, along with the gradual establishment of Christianity in

Europe, a widespread hatred of cats developed during the Middle Ages. People believed that the cat, especially the black cat, was the form taken by the devil himself or by his witch servants. Because of this, countless cats were burned upon pyres or otherwise persecuted. As a result, rodents were allowed to proliferate unchecked, causing widespread epidemics.

In spite of the cruel persecution launched by the church, people soon began to realize the cat's beneficial influence upon both the household and on farming. As soon as the cat's usefulness was appreciated, a gradual change in public attitude became noticeable. The cat regained its former popularity, and keeping a cat became commonplace among peasants, nobles and clergymen alike. Deliberately killing a cat was punishable by law. In some places, the laws of the land even decreed that cats must be kept. There is historical evidence that cats used to be favourite pets of many monarchs, popes and cardinals. For example, French Cardinal Richelieu is said to have kept at least 14 cats at one time, playing with them every morning. Cats were faithful and cherished companions of numerous statesmen, artists and politicians, such as Leonardo da Vinci, Vladimir Ilich Lenin and Winston Churchill. Today, cats enjoy extreme popularity in most parts of the world.

The first longhaired cats were probably brought to Europe from the Near East in the 16th century. Until this time, only shorthaired cats with common coat colours and pattern combinations were normally available. They were similar in appearance to the typical tabby 'alley' cats known today. There was no regulated cat breeding and proliferation took place without human interference. It was not until the second half of the last century that breeders took an interest in the growing number of different body types and coat colours, and eventually decided to maintain the distinctive traits by systematic breeding.

Deliberate crossing began, allied to the selection of the animals most suitable for breeding — particularly specimens corresponding to a particular standard of points. Special cat shows were held in order to compare and assess the animals which had been bred. The National Cat Show was the first benched cat show in the world. It was held in 1871 in London, exhibiting a total number of 170 cats. The show met with a great response, and marked the start of a new period in the relationship between man and the cat. Over the years, many new breeds and colour varieties have been developed. This had led to the establishment of clubs and societies designed to promote the many different types of cats, most of which also publish specialized literature. Cat breeding also continues to attract an ever-increasing number of novices.

The cat's body

The domestic cat has reached an advanced stage of development, although its basic anatomical structure has remained much the same as that of other members of the cat family. This is most probably due to the fact that the cat was domesticated much later than most of other domestic animals, which for many thousands of years were reared by humans. Let us look at the cat's dental structure, which is one of the most important developmental features. The dental formula of the domestic cat is practically the same as that of most felids living in the wild. Even among individual breeds of the domestic cat there are only minor differences in the proportions of the body organs. This contrasts with different breeds of dog, where there is often great variation in the size and shape of the body organs.

Individual cat breeds differ from each other by characteristics known as type and conformation. The type encompasses distinguishing features such as the length of the nose and its inclination, the shape of the cheeks and the chin, as well as the features which are not dependent on the bone internal skeleton such as the size and the form of the ears and the size and location of eyes. These differences may, however, be very slight in some feline breeds.

Relatively small differences are similarly found in the conformation of the body, tail and legs. Particular variations will be

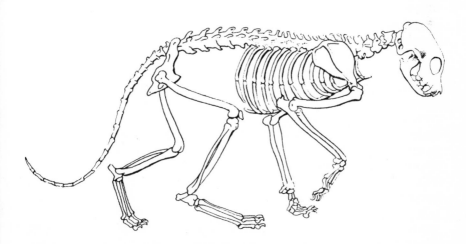

The structure of the cat's skeleton is similar to that of other mammals, in particular predators. It is composed of about 240 bones.

Three hair types: guard hair (1), awn hair (2) and down or wool hair (3).

1 2 3

discussed in the pictorial section of the book under separate breeds. These distinguishing features have been clearly defined in the standards of points, or show standards, which relate to each type of cat. Standards serve primarily as guidance for breeders in their work. When assessing cats, show judges are also obliged to adhere to current standards, although the overall appearance and bearing of the cat will also be taken into account.

The cat's body is covered with a coat, except for the nose leather, lips, paw pads, anal and genital areas and an inner part of the ear flap (pinna). The coat is composed of separate hairs growing in clusters called dermatomes. With the exceptions of a few coat types which will be discussed later, each dermatome contains three different types of hair: guard, awn and down. There is usually a single guard hair in the dermatome, which is longer and stiffer than the others. The awn hairs in a dermatome are usually characterized by being slightly wider at the tip. Down, or wool, hairs are softer and shorter than the guard and awn hairs. There are about twice as many down hairs as there are awn hairs in each dermatome.

Pigment granules located in the hairs produce the various colours of the feline coat. The heredity of colouring in cats is determined by genetic laws. These laws were formulated in the second half of the last century on the basis of research carried out by the Austrian geneticist J. G. Mendel, the abbot of the Augustinian monastery in Brün, Austria, now Brno, Czechoslovakia.

In spite of intense study, heredity in cats has not been fully explored yet, and so far geneticists have acquired only incomplete knowledge. Little is known about the heredity of traits such as dentition, eye colour and the size and shape of other body parts. (Heredity of coat colours will be discussed under separate colour varieties.)

10

Let us examine some of the basic facts of genetics. During cell division, the chromatin differentiates into threadlike structures called chromosomes. Genes, or units of heredity, are carried along them. The cat has 18 autosomal chromosome pairs determining the inheritance of all traits and qualities, with the exception of the animal's sex, which is determined by two sex chromosomes called gonosomes. The part of the chromosome on which a particular gene is located is called the gene's locus. Both the locus and the gene are referred to by the same letter. Genes determining coat colours are carried on the same pairs of autosomal chromosomes, except for the gene determining red colour, which is carried on the X chromosome determining the animal's sex. Alternative forms of a gene are known as alleles. Alleles can be dominant (in which case they are depicted by capital or upper-case letters) or recessive (symbolized by small or lower-case letters). An identical pair of alleles on a chromosome AA for a particular characteristic is termed homozygous, while a pair of dissimilar alleles Aa is called heterozygous.

Geneticists believe that coat colouring is determined by genes positioned on eight loci (A, B, C, D, O, S, T, W). The tabby pattern is determined by the dominant allele A or agouti-factor. The agouti-factor is linked with the alleles positioned on the locus T, which determines the Abyssinian pattern as well as the patterns of other tabbies: ticked or Abyssinian type; spotted and mackerel and classic (blotched or marbled). The homozygous allele a determines self (solid) colour of the hair. It conceals the presence of the locus T alleles. This is known as epistasis, or masking.

In some breeds, varieties with coloured ends to the hairs occur. This is known as tipping. Its occurrence is determined by the presence of the inhibiting gene I. If the allele i is homozygous, hairs have a uniform colour along their length.

Dilute genes constitute another group of genes. In a homozygous state, allele b on the locus B 'dilutes' the basic black to a chocolate (chestnut) colour, while the allele d on the locus D 'dilutes' black to blue. If the alleles b and d are both present in the homozygous state, a lilac (lavender) colour is produced.

Acromelanic colouring is a distinctive darker colour on the face, ears, feet and tail, which is found in some breeds with points, such as the Persian Colourpoint, the Birmans and the Siamese. It is caused by the presence of one of the alleles c^s on the locus C. Alleles in this series can occur in alternative forms. One of them causes the above-mentioned acromelanic colouring, another determines the colouring of the Burmese, while other alleles carry different types of colouring in albinos.

Pure white coat colour is determined by the allele W on the locus W. Provided the allele occurs in the heterozygous state, colours other than white can be passed on to the offspring as well. White spotting or patches are determined by the dominant allele S on the locus S. In that case, discrete white spots are visible on the feline coat. This is known as piebald spotting.

The red coat colour is determined by the presence of the allele O on the chromosome X, which determines a cat's sex. Cats carrying alleles for red colour on both sex chromosomes XX are homozygous and self red. Tortoiseshell cats are heterozygous, carrying the allele O on one of the X chromosomes and the allele o on the other. This is because the rule of dominance and recessiveness does not apply in this particular case. When homozygous, allele d dilutes the red to a cream colour, and the tortoiseshell to a blue-cream colour. The allele O on the X chromosome causes red coloration in male cats, while the allele o brings about black coat colour. Since males have only one X chromosome, no 'true' tortoiseshell male cats occur although some sterile males have been known. The same applies to the blue-cream.

Perhaps the greatest diversity among the breeds can be found by examining the feline head. The most remarkable differences can be seen particularly in the underlying bone structure of the skull, but also in other non-skeletal traits, which are consequently more variable.

Cat breeds can be distinguished according to the head type. The most perfectly rounded head shape is found in the longhairs (Persians). The roundness is supported by broad cheek bones, a short nose and a broad, massive chin. In the British, European, Chartreux and Manx breeds the skull is rather massive, though not as perfectly round as in the longhairs. There are also differences in the skeletal structure to be found among the breeds listed, although these are not very conspicuous. In addition, the breeds listed display a large nose, and their cheek bones and chin display varying degrees of development. Other breeds have a narrower skull in the chin area, and a longer nose. The narrowest skull with a wedged chin is found among the Siamese and Oriental cats.

In the area between the nose and the forehead a delicate notch, distinctly changing the direction of the profile, is found in varying degrees of development according to the breed. This is called a nose break or stop. An extremely deep break is found in the Peke-faced Persian (see pages 55 and 64).

The cat's permanent dentition comprises 16 teeth in the upper jaw (six incisors, two canines, six premolars and two molars) and 14 in the lower jaw, with four premolars only. This number of teeth applies to all felines except for the cheetah. The presence of the nose break is

A profile of the longhair (Persian); a distinct notch can be seen in the area between the nose and forehead. This is known as the nose break or stop.

The head of the Burmese cat: a muzzle pinch can be seen on the lower part of the cheeks.

likely to exert influence on dental deformations. That is to say, an undershot jaw is frequently encountered with the peke-faced breeds as well as with other animals with a highly developed nose break (see pages 184—5). Unlike dogs, which often show a reduction in the number of teeth, no such deformations or variability of teeth number are found among cats.

In the area intermediate between the lower part of the cheeks and the whiskers (vibrissae), a notch of variable depth is developed in some breeds. This is called a muzzle pinch. As the muzzle pinch distorts an otherwise fluent line, its presence is regarded as undesirable in breeds having the rounded profile contours from the ear tips to the chin required by the show standard.

As regards the general structure of the skeleton, no differences among the breeds can be observed. However, show standards sometimes distinguish between particular body sizes, leg proportions and paw shapes. The only principal exception is constituted by the members of the Manx breed which have undergone essential changes in the skeletal structure of the body and limbs.

Certain deviations in the tail are also found in some breeds. Except for the Manx, with lacking or reduced caudal (tail) vertebrae, a constant number of 20 to 27 vertebrae has been preserved in all breeds. The only variability is found in the shape and size of the vertebrae. However, deformations of terminal caudal vertebrae are encountered quite frequently, resulting in a kinked tail. Kinks can be seen or felt, the deformations being passed on to the progeny. In the past, kinks were acceptable, but currently cats with their tails kinked are not selected for further breeding.

Caudal vertebrae help the cat to maintain balance. Just try to picture how a falling cat regulates its fall by 'steering' with its tail. When walking, especially out of doors, the cat corrects its balance with its tail, thus helping each foot to land softly on the ground. In addition, the tail often indicates a cat's mood or feelings.

Being a highly developed vertebrate, it is only natural that the cat has well-developed sense organs. The centre of activity for these organs is of course the brain. In the cat, the ratio of brain weight to body weight is greater than in most other animals — some predators included. Although some feline features and qualities have changed through the influence of domestication, the anatomical structure of the sense organs has remained largely unaffected when compared with felids living in the wild. In domestic cats, the senses closely connected with hunting as a way of obtaining food have remained highly developed.

Consequently, hearing and vision are the cat's most perfectly developed senses. With its relatively large and erect ears, the cat is able to hear even very faint rustlings, and from them can locate prey with great accuracy. Like other animals, the cat is able to move its pinnae, thus directing its ears towards the sound. The cat responds primarily to high-pitched sounds as high as 65 kilohertz, while human hearing has its limit at 17 kilohertz. The cat is even able to detect the sounds by which mice communicate. Perfect vision helps the cat to calculate the correct distance to leap when attempting to grab its prey.

Within the cat's inner ear is an organ contributing to balance. When the cat rolls over, the vestibular apparatus helps it to return to a normal position — as it does when falling from a great height. The tail, used to counteract any overbalance, guarantees a safe landing on all fours.

The eyes are set forward on the head, enabling the cat to have an equal, overlapping visual field with each eye. Felids, like humans, have three-dimensional vision. The cat's eyes are less mobile than those of man, but this disadvantage is largely compensated for by head movements. Feline eyes are similar in their structure to those of other mammals. In contrast to dogs, cats are able to distinguish several colours (red, green and blue). This is a clear indication that they have colour vision. However, the cat probably cannot focus very well on stationary, close-up objects. This is most likely due to the curvature of the cornea.

Feline eyes have a remarkable capability for narrowing and dilating the pupils. In the middle of each pupil there are retractile muscles which regulate the amounts of light passing through the eye. In bright light, the pupil narrows to a slit, while in dim light it may open to form a circle with a diameter of as much as 12 mm ($^1/_2$ in). This indicates that the cat like other predators is able to see in the dark much better than any other mammal. Nevertheless, even cats are not able to see in complete darkness. New-born kittens initially have blue eyes, since there are no yellow-orange pigment crystals deposited in their corneas yet. The crystals do not begin to appear there until between the first and third months of age, thus changing the colour of a kitten's eyes.

The third eyelid, also known as the haw or the nictitating membrane, can usually be spotted in the inner corner of the eye. The haw is a thin fold of skin, helping to moisten the eye surface and keep it free of dust. This is also the reason why cats are known to blink less frequently than any other animals or humans.

The cat responds to chemical stimuli in the air by means of its acute sense of smell. The cat has a highly sensitive olfactory mucosa near the nasal partition. However, when compared with the dog, the cat has a poorer sense of smell. This is best observed when food is offered: it is sniffed much more thoroughly by the cat than the dog. This may be partly due to the cat's higher degree of cautiousness, although a comparison between the two anatomical structures of the brain shows a distinct difference in the size of the olfactory centre. This is because smell is the most developed of the dog's senses.

The cat's taste organs are located at the sides and base of the tongue as well as on the soft palate. These receptors respond even to minute concentrations of substances. It has been observed, however, that the responsiveness of the taste organs to different stimuli is not very developed in cats.

The cat is also able to detect different kinds of external stimuli and respond to them. For example, it is known that a cat can find its way across unknown terrain by responding to the Earth's magnetic field and the position of the Sun. The cat's ability to sense, and make use of these phenomena so far remains unexplained. Neither is it fully understood how cats anticipate an imminent earthquake, changes in atmospheric pressure or even know that their owner is going on holiday the next day.

The cat's main organ of touch are its whiskers or vibrissae. Their roots extend deep into the dermis, close to the network of nerve fibre endings. Whiskers are found mainly on the cat's head, near the mouth and around the eyes. Movements of the whiskers enable the cat to balance skilfully and to orient itself generally. The whiskers also provide other kinds of information. For example, they allow the cat to hunt for its prey at night. The whiskers do not moult like the cat's coat, since they grow continuously and wear down with use. As well as the whiskers, the hairless nose pad and foot pads are quite sensitive to touch. The areas sensitive to touch are among the first to investigate any new objects which the cat encounters. First, the object is cautiously approached, then it is thoroughly examined by a paw and eventually sniffed.

How cats reproduce

During the breeding season, an ability to form mature eggs capable of being fertilized, as well as ripe sperm, appears in all species. The particular age of a cat's sexual maturity depends on the breed, sex, nutrition and quality of care as well as on environmental and other factors. Like other domestic animals, cats achieve a sexual maturity before their physical development is completed. In the cat this occurs between seven and nine months of age.

The regular cycles of breeding activity in female cats are called heat or oestrus. In domestic and pedigree cats oestrus occurs throughout the year; the intervals between the cycles vary according to the cat's physical condition and the season of the year. The shortest intervals occur in spring. Each oestrus lasts on average six to eight days. After a cat has been mated, the outward signs tend to disappear within 24 hours. Tom (male) cats have no regular sexual cycle, being able to mate at any time of the year. The heat, which is usually accompanied by different kinds of sounds and movements, is a manifestation of processes also taking place in the female's sex organs. A queen (female cat in season) usually mews wistfully, rolls on her back and rubs against objects and people's feet. She is restless, trying to escape out of doors. All these symptoms signal a preparation for ovulation (the release of eggs from the ovaries into the oviducts). When comparing a queen and a female dog in heat, we can see that a bitch has a bloody vaginal discharge during this period, followed by ovulation. In the cat, ovulation takes place only if mating actually occurs. If no mating occurs, the eggs remain in the ovaries, shrivel up and are absorbed. Then, preparation for the next heat takes place.

Cats are, by nature, solitary animals. However, the barrier between two individuals must be broken in order for mating to occur to preserve the feline population. Thus, prior to mating, a special courtship ritual has developed, the fundamental features of which are the same for all cats.

The character of courtship varies, however. Much depends on whether or not the courtship occurs between cats which already know each other, or whether it is between a pair of unacquainted cats. Mating takes place more quickly between acquainted cats. When meeting an unknown stud a queen is reluctant for a while, giving the impression that she wants to escape from him, while looking for him to follow at the same time. The tom cat patiently keeps sitting near her, crooning in a soft voice and making inviting gestures for mating.

Eventually, the queen shows her consent by crouching down, slightly lifting up her hindquarters and moving her tail to one side. The tom cat grasps her by the scruff of the neck and mounts her, front legs first. During the sexual act, the queen emits a deep, monotonous sound. Genital contact lasts only a few seconds. The tom cat then jumps off, and the queen rolls over and remains like this for a while. After some time she turns back on all fours and mating is usually repeated several times more.

Pregnancy, or gestation, is the period from fertilization to the birth. In cats, it lasts on average between 58 and 71 days, the most common length of pregnancy being about 63 to 66 days. Up to the sixtieth day of pregnancy, the female cat behaves just as usual. However, about three to four days prior to labour, a sudden change in her behaviour occurs. The body temperature drops to 37.5 °C (99.5 °F) — sometimes even below this. The mother-to-be becomes restless, tends to move less, greatly enjoys petting and follows her master everywhere. These are unmistakable signs of imminent birth. The onset of labour is usually indicated by signs of discomfort and extreme restlessness. The delivery itself begins by the outflow of the foetal water followed by contractions; the first kitten is produced within approximately one hour. Non-pedigree domestic cats usually cope with birth without any human assistance. However, it would be false to assume that all cats can do so. Sometimes a cat, especially a pedigree variety, is so dependent upon her master that she can delay the birth if her owner is away from home. On the other hand, there are some cats which wait for a moment of solitude in order not to be bothered by anyone. The cat's individualism shows itself even here.

The cat often purrs during labour, although the purr is quite different from the sound emitted during moments of contentment. It is a similar sound to the purring made by a nervous cat or a cat in pain. Intervals between the birth of each kitten vary from ten minutes to several hours. A kitten is born within one or two minutes, most frequently head first. After the birth, the cat bites through the umbilical cord and releases the kitten from the amnion. She then licks it all over and gives it a massage with her tongue to dry the kitten and to stimulate the lungs to breathe. The queen then eats her placenta. The reason for this is thought to be not only because of feline cleanliness, but also because the placenta contains vital nutrients and hormones, facilitating the delivery of further kittens in the litter.

Kittens are born with their eyelids sealed shut. They usually do not open until 7 to 14 days after birth. In only a few breeds of pedigree cats is it usual for the kittens to open their eyelids earlier.

Premature kittens, born before the sixtieth day of pregnancy, have only a small chance of surviving. For although a slightly lower birth weight can be quite easily compensated for by extra care, premature kittens usually have not developed a sucking reflex. They do not know how to suckle or swallow and cannot find their mother's milk nipples. Apart from this, they are not able to retain the warmth of their own bodies. Growth of the coat has not been completed, and some of the key points of the skeleton have not developed fully.

The mother's milk is the basis of the kitten's nutrition. The queen's mammary glands become active during the second half of the pregnancy. By this time, it is possible to press out a few drops of colostrum from the nipples, which are slightly swollen. Their functioning becomes established either a few days prior to the delivery, or during the labour, or — at the latest — by the first sucking of kittens. Young kittens suckle almost continuously, only taking short breaks to have a sleep.

Kittens of both sexes weigh about 80 to 120 g/3 to 4 oz (the average being 99 g), regardless of the breed. The weight is doubled within a week. Later, the kittens gain about 100 g (4 oz) each week. By the end of the second month, the average weight of a kitten is about 500 to 1 300 g (1 to 3 lb), depending on the breed. From the third week on male kittens gain weight a little more rapidly than female kittens. At this time kittens weigh about a quarter of their adult weight while at three months they have already gained a third of their future weight.

From about three to four weeks of age, the mother's milk should be gradually replaced by an adult diet. The exact time that this should occur depends on many circumstances, primarily on the condition of the nursing queen's health and the number of kittens in the litter. However, weaning can be started by this time anyway, though the queen may still have enough milk. Kittens may be weaned at first with evaporated milk diluted with an equal volume of hot water. Some breeders add a little cereal suitable for human babies with honey, mixing to produce a thick cream-like consistency. A little later meat can be added to the diet. Well minced or scraped raw or boiled meat is forked into small mounds to encourage the kittens to eat after they are given the taste by having their lips lightly smeared with the offered food. Two weeks after the initial weaning process has begun, new foods may be introduced such as creamed chicken and white fish, cottage cheese and canned products specially formulated for kittens. As some breeds may be allergic to milk and/or eggs, care should be exercised in feeding these.

The cat's diet and daily care

It has already been said that cats are highly individual, always making their own choice, even for food. One cat may completely dislike another's favourite dish and vice versa. Each breeder has acquired a special experience of his own and therefore questions about cats' diet are quite difficult to answer. First and foremost we have to realize that a cat cannot be fed solely on household scraps. Cats should be given a special food, prepared with constituents specially designed for their nutritional requirements. Many ingredients in human food, particularly items such as spices, are harmful to cats. Daily allowances depend upon food quality as well as a cat's weight and general health. The quality of food is related to its energy content, which must be utilized by a cat from its daily allowance.

Major food components are proteins, fats and sugars. Each of these substances has a different energy content. Cats have a particularly great need for proteins. They constitute the basis of their diet. Proteins are of both animal and vegetable type. Meat is a particularly good source of animal proteins. Consequently, meat should be the cat's basic food. The cat is a strictly adapted carnivore, unable to survive without eating meat, which forms the major component in the cat's diet. Although the feline diet should be well balanced, meat, either raw or cooked, should always be present. Other sources of quality animal proteins are eggs, milk and milk products. Vegetable proteins, contained for example in oatmeal, form another important constituent in the feline diet. However, they are difficult for the cat to digest. Therefore, vegetable proteins should be added to animal proteins in limited amounts only, since the cat is able to assimilate and digest only a small part of their energy content.

Until recently it was not recommended to include fats in the cat's diet. Today, however, we know that cats should be given reasonable amounts of fats regularly. The calorie content of fats is twice as high as that of proteins and sugars. Furthermore most essential vitamins are fat-soluble. It follows, therefore, that vitamins are utilized better when fats are added to the cat's diet — preferably mixed directly into a meal in a liquid state.

Sugars are least beneficial to the cat's nutrition. Fortunately, cats do not consume much sugar, although they gradually become used to it and their requirements for sugar are constantly growing as a consequence of their association with man. When eaten in small amounts sugars do no harm. However, too much sugar causes obesity in cats.

Apart from the three main sources of the nutrients already mentioned, cats need other substances as well. These substances do not increase the energy intake, but they are vital for the maintenance of good metabolism and for the cat's health in general. These are vitamins, trace elements and mineral substances. From the great number of vitamins existing, the following are essential fot the cat's nutrition: A, B complex, D, E and H. When preparing a cat's food, one should therefore use raw materials rich in the vitamins listed, plus trace elements and minerals. These are, particularly, liver, fish oil, milk, yeast and egg yolk. However, one should remember that an excess of vitamins, particularly vitamin A, can be harmful to the cat.

At least minute amounts of trace elements and minerals are needed for the proper metabolism of every living creature, the cat included. The need for these substances varies with the animal, being dependent upon many circumstances, such as an animal's stage of development, or period of possible convalescence, etc.

Finally, the folowing items should never be offered to a cat: chocolate and other sweets, cocoa, alcohol, smoked meat, sausages and salamis, spiced pâtés, pastries, lard, bacon, pickles, peanuts, jams and marmalades and preserved fruits. Coffee should be offered exceptionally as a medicine in pathological cases such as collapse and then only under instructions from the vet.

A correct diet is really a matter of common sense. The portions as well as the type of food should be considered so that the cat becomes neither obese nor skinny. Cats should be well-proportioned and compact, which is further specified by particular standards of points for the particular breed. Since it is in the nature of domestic cats that they never over-eat, obesity is not a typical feature of their own doing. Therefore, an obese cat is almost always the fault of the owner, who is not able to assess a cat's calorie consumption, thus causing its obesity by systematic over-feeding.

Do not forget that a cat should always have enough liquid to drink. This means that fresh water in a clean bowl should always be available.

How many times a day should a cat be fed? Humans and cats alike should be accustomed to eating at particular hours of the day. The cat becomes used to these intervals as soon as weaning has been started, and these are preserved throughout its life. Until four months of age, kittens should be fed five or six times a day, preferably according to a scheduled feeding programme. Intervals between meals should be as regular as possible, plus an extra overnight interval should be observed. At the age of four to six months, the kitten itself will reduce the number of meals to four a day. Between six and 12 months, the number of feedings decreases to three, while an adult cat, older than one year, should be fed only twice a day. Feeding a cat only once a day has not proved sufficient. The cat's daily allowance should be divided into two feedings, the food being offered at about 8 a.m. and 6 p.m. These hours approximately coincide with the periods of the cat's increased activity and, consequently, with the increased need for food.

Food should be offered in a clean bowl and left there for about ten minutes. Within this time a cat will probably eat most of the food offered. The rest of the food should be removed after ten minutes and stored in a refrigerator until the next feeding. The bowl should be thoroughly washed with warm water.

Pregnant and elderly cats should be offered equal or slightly larger amounts of food than normal adults. Their daily allowance should, however, be divided into more feedings. A lactating cat can be given unrestricted amounts of food. If the meal is eaten promptly, more food can be added. It is recommended, however, to divide the daily requirement into several meals during the day so as not to 'overload' the digestive system.

Proper nutrition is not the only thing an owner should offer his cat. Other requirements can be classed in two groups: routine care and other prerequisites for keeping a cat healthy.

A breeder wishing to produce a first-class pedigree animal should attend primarily to the cat's coat. Regular combing and grooming is indispensable. In additon, the coat should be exposed to sufficient amounts of sun and fresh air. A dry powder shampoo is frequently used as a dirt and grease remover, when arranging the coat of long-hairs and semi-longhairs. The shampoo should be rubbed into the coat and then brushed out carefully. Shampooing makes the coat fluffy and gives a soft and supple look. Grooming of shorthairs is much simpler. Occasional grooming is usually sufficient, preferably during the period of coat shedding. The cat is made to look sleek by smoothing the coat with a leather glove. Some cats, however, have different requirements for coat care. This will be mentioned, if necessary, under the separate breeds and varieties in the pictorial section.

Exposure to sunlight is a prerequisite for the cat's good health. It is vital for cats at the juvenile stage, when vitamin D is needed in large amounts. An oily secretion called sebum is excreted by tiny sebaceous glands located in the skin. Sebum contains cholesterol, which sunlight converts to vitamin D. The cat then takes in the vitamin D by licking its coat.

The cat licks itself mainly in the course of caring for its coat, which is periodically shed, especially in spring and autumn. The cat removes the dead hair with its abrasive tongue. However, the hairs are swallowed at the time. They collect in the stomach and form hairballs. These hairballs are not passed through the intestines but are ejected via the mouth from time to time. This should not be considered as pathological vomiting, since it provides merely a mechanical means of cleansing the stomach.

Cats do not usually require baths. A bath is needed only when a cat is very dirty, or before the show, provided the coat is too greasy to be brushed with a dry shampoo.

The rest of the care involves regular checking of the cat's condition. Its teeth should be examined, and its eyes and ears should be cleaned. Excessive tear production can be removed with a clean piece of soft white cloth soaked in a solution of boric acid. Dirty ears should be carefully cleaned with dry cotton buds or swabs but these must not be inserted down into the ear canal.

At home, a cat should be found a suitable place to make its bed. Although a cat usually makes its own choice for the place to rest — and, most frequently, this is not a bed you prepared for it — providing such a place gives your cat a sense of security and cosiness. It should be placed in a quiet, draught-free position, preferably close to some form of heating. A litter tray is another vital piece of equipment. This should be placed away from the bed a little, and should be cleaned regularly, since most cats do not use a dirty litter tray. If the

Although a cat's bed can be made of any suitable material, one of the best types is an airy wicker basket with sides of medium height. It can be lined with a pillow or blanket and should be sited in a draught-free area away from the general bustle of the household.

A plastic container is best for the litter tray, since it is easy to disinfect. Fired clay granules or tiny paper scraps are most commonly used as a filling nowadays. Alternatively the tray can be left empty. Sand is not suitable as it tends to stick to the cat's paws.

tray is often dirty, a cat will get into the habit of using other places, which is not very convenient for the owner. Plastic litter trays are most suitable, as they are easy to wash with hot water and can be occasionally disinfected. The tray should be filled with fired clay granules, which is a common commercial litter. It need not be thrown away after each use.

The cat's claws grow continually, and this is why the cat has to sharpen them constantly. The cat which is allowed to go outdoors sharpens its claws by walking on rough surfaces in addition to scratching on various objects when marking its boundaries. Scratching deposits a secretion from sweat glands on the paw pads and leaves scent marking on visible scratches. Indoors, a cat does not have to mark its boundaries, but its claws keep on growing just the same. Therefore a cat should be given a scratching post such as a piece of log or a square of carpet mounted on wood. There are

Cats constantly need to strop their claws, and they should be given a suitable scratching post at home. They often take a fancy to a softwood log or any other rough object attached to a post.

different kinds of scratching posts available on the market. Most cats quickly grasp what all these things are for and soon take to using them. Some cats like to sharpen their nails soon after they wake up in the morning and consequently their scratching post should be placed within easy reach of their bed.

What the cat needs most, and what no cat fancier should underestimate, is emotional attachment. Providing all the necessary care mentioned above is not enough; the cat must be able to establish a bond of affection with its owner. A breeder or owner should always be on friendly terms with his cats, attend to them, pet them, pat their coats and talk to them. Overall, he should not neglect their personalities. Nor should he worry whether or not his efforts are in vain, since the cat will pay the affection back many times over.

Keeping cats healthy

Assuming a balanced diet and a stress-free evironment are provided, most cats are remarkably healthy animals. Sometimes, however, changes in the cat's health can occur. Routine check-ups can help prevent the spread of various diseases or minimize their effects in time. Every breeder or owner should get used to his cat's monthly health check-ups. You do not have to take the cat to the vet for this purpose. A vet should be called only in case some serious departures from the normal health condition are observed.

A systematic, step-by-step examination can be done in the following manner. First of all, you should pay attention to the general appearance of the coat, which should not be limp. On the contrary, in breeds where a close-lying coat is required by the standard, a bristly coat undoubtedly signals a disorder. The cat's eyes can tell something about its health, too. They shouldn't be dull, hazy or yellowish, and they should be free of any discharge. You should make sure that the cat doesn't show any signs of bad breath. No yellowish tinge should be found on the mucus membrane. Now the whole head has been checked over, except for the ears. They should be examined for inflammation or ear mites. They should be perfectly clean without excessive wax. Increased secretion of wax may indicate infestation by ear mites. The cat's claws should be checked to ensure that they have not penetrated the flesh and to examine for any signs of damage. The cat's anus should be examined, as well as the colour and consistency of the urine and stools. An irritated and reddened anal area may betray internal parasites. If possible, the cat's temperature, pulse rate and respiration rate should be taken regularly, while the cat is lying quietly at rest. Any departure from the normal conditions may signal health disorders. The normal respiration rate of an adult cat is 20 to 30 breaths per minute, the pulse rate 100 to 140 beats per minute; the body temperature fluctuates between 38 and 39 °C (100—102 °F).

Cleanliness of the cat and its surroundings is another preventive precaution which should be taken by an owner or breeder. This includes different kinds of routine disinfection, namely the thorough washing and cleaning of the most frequently used items of cat equipment. In common practice, many disinfectants are used, such as chloroamine, which is not harmful to cats. There are, however, other substances, such as phenol, acetone, lysol, naphthalene, creosote and others, which are extremely harmful to cats, for they cause poisoning, eczemas and different kinds of nervous shocks. An owner or breeder should therefore prevent the cat coming into contact not only with these chemicals, but also with other preparations commonly used for exterminating insects as well as for cultivating house plants (herbicides and fertilizers).

There are many symptoms which enable an illness in a cat to be identified quite easily. Some of them are very obvious, others are less so. All, however, are spotted primarily by owners who know their cats very well and carry out regular preventive check-ups. Most disorders manifest themselves through changes in temperature. Any rise or drop in temperature signals the presence of infection in the cat's body. Checking the cat's temperature should be carried out with a rectal thermometer; a rise in body temperature cannot be judged by merely touching the tip of the cat's nose. Additional symptoms of illness include excessive drinking, vomiting, salivation, lack of appetite, a swollen abdomen, diarrhoea or constipation, blood in the urine, a foul smell on the breath or excessive tear production.

Before the cat is taken to the vet, it should, above all, be kept calm. To prevent injury, it should be put in an appropriate box or a wicker basket with a soft lining (remember to provide a sufficient air supply). Alternatively, the cat may be covered in a warm blanket and left in a quiet, draught-free and dimly-lit place.

Vaccination against different kinds of infectious diseases constitutes an elementary precaution. Panleukopaenia (FIE or feline infectious enteritis) is among the most dangerous feline ailments which can be prevented by proper vaccination. (After vaccination, specific antibodies are formed in the organism, which protect the cat from further infections for a certain period of time). Panleukopaenia and rabies are quite commonly spread among feral and stray cats, although rabies does not occur in Britain. Unless the cat was vaccinated in advance both infectious diseases are fatal. Should the germ of the disease enter the vaccinated animal, the symptoms of the disease either do not show themselves at all, or the course of the disease is much milder and the cat recovers.

FIE occurs chiefly in cats allowed to go outdoors freely, roaming all day and coming home only for a meal or to sleep. Furthermore, these animals can often transmit to their owners different kinds of parasites as well as germs of serious diseases (zoonoses) such as fleas and, consequently, some species of tapeworms, mites, TBC, toxoplasmosis, salmonellosis, leptospirosis and some fungal skin diseases.

Cats which are allowed to roam at will are also at risk from road traffic, which causes death to thousands of animals every year. Those who care for their cats never allow them to stray. Instead, they give them a comfortable and safe home and everything needed for a healthy and long life.

Cat fancies and shows

Pedigree cat breeders join clubs, associations and unions in order to improve their breeds, exchange experience and spread information on breeding activities. The first cat club in the world, the National Cat Club, was founded in 1887 in Great Britain. At present, there are two bodies representing British breeders — the Governing Council of the Cat Fancy (GCCF) and the Cat Association of Britain (CA). The GCCF oversees other clubs, including the National Cat Club.

In the United States a number of independent cat associations exist. The largest, the Cat Fanciers' Association (CFA), was founded in 1906. Each club keeps its own registration records, grants recognition to new breeds and varieties and specifies breed standards of perfection. A similar system operates in Japan and other countries with highly developed pedigree cat breeding programmes.

The European and some of the overseas cat fanciers' associations are affiliated with the main international organization, Fédération Internationale Féline (FIFe), which was founded in 1949. At present, the organization includes among its number the cat fanciers' associations of Australia, Belgium, Brazil, Czechoslovakia, Denmark, Finland, France, the Netherlands, Italy, Liechtenstein, Luxembourg, Hungary, Malaysia, Mexico, Norway, the Federal Republic of Germany, Austria, San Marino, Singapore, Spain, Sweden and Switzerland.

All cat fanciers' associations affiliated with the FIFe are obliged to adhere to the status of the organization and maintain current standards. Each association keeps its own pedigree records, registering members' cats and issuing certificates. A pedigree certificate is a document recording a newborn kitten's ancestry in a pedigree record of a particular association. It also recognizes the possibility of further breeding, according to requirements specified by each association separately. The certificate records at least three generations of an animal's ancestors. In addition to proper pedigree records, each association keeps an experimental or preliminary record, which encompasses those cats, corresponding to show standard requirements, but not verifying three generations of ancestors.

Cat shows are one of the most effective ways of promoting interest in cats. International cat shows allow the breeders to compare the level of breeding in their own and other countries. Exhibited animals are assessed by qualified judges.

Exhibited cats are divided into separate classes according to the breed, variety, sex, age and, occasionally, according to the number of awards so far acquired. Each cat is assessed according to its qualities as laid down in its breed standard. Each cat is given a certain number of points according to its qualities and is certified as excellent, very good or good.

The GCCF winner of an open adult class can be awarded a challenge certificate. If a cat wins three challenge certificates at three separate shows under three different judges, it is allowed to enter a 'champion of champions' class. Here it can win a grand challenge certificate, three of which are needed to become a grand champion.

The European system is similar to that of the GCCF in some respects. The winner (which must be more than ten months old) of an open class is awarded, apart from the title 'excellent 1', a *Certificat d'Aptitude au Championnat* (CAC). Three such titles allow a cat to enter the class for champions only, where a winner is awarded *Certificat d'Aptitude au Championnat International de Beauté* (CACIB). Three wins at this level qualify a cat for international champion status. The International Champions compete in a special class where the winner can obtain, apart from the note 'excellent 1', the title CAGCIB. If a cat wins this title six times it is awarded the title of Grand Champion International ('Gr. Int. Ch.') and is allowed to enter a higher class. There, apart from 'excellent 1', such an outstanding animal can obtain the title CACE and after winning this title nine times it is qualified to the title European Champion. A cat may be selected for 'best in show' or 'best of breed' awards.

Neuters have a parallel system of titles from premier CAP (*Certifi-*

cat d'Aptitude au Premier) to international grand premier. For a neutered cat the title corresponding to CAGCIB is CAGPIB and the title CAPE corresponds to CACE. A neutered cat cannot, however, be nominated for 'best in breed' award, it can only be entitled to the title of a best neuter of breed or variety, or a best neuter in show.

Overall, breeds are classified as Longhair, Semi-longhair, Short-hair, and Siamese and Oriental. According to FIFe standards, each breed and variety has its exact code number and designation. At present (up to June 1, 1986), an overall number of 432 breeds and varieties of pedigree cats has been recognized. This number includes 95 longhair, 40 semi-longhair, 238 shorthair and 59 Siamese and Oriental breeds and varieties.

Colour Illustrations

Black Longhair (Black Persian)

Persian cats or longhairs are among the most popular of cat breeds worldwide. Their pensive expression is caused by the unique structure of the head. The roundness of the head is complemented by full cheeks, a rounded chin, a very short nose with a distinct break and, particularly, by small ears with rounded tips, set far apart. The eyes are quite large, rounded, and set wide apart. The body of Persian cats is short and cobby, set low on stocky legs, and the tail is short with a full brush.

All colour varieties of Persian cats are descended from the original Angora cats (2), which were bred from longhaired mutants of shorthairs. If, by deliberate crossing, the Persian breed is not maintained, it has a tendency to vanish quickly. Thus, the offspring may show the original features of Angoras on some of their body parts — such as a longer nose, more strongly wedged chin, narrower cheeks, or longer ears, trunk and tail than are found in purebred Persians. Although the Persians (3) and the Angoras (4) show a similarly longhaired coat, there is a difference between them. The hairs of the Persian's coat are as much as 15 cm (6 inches) long and much softer, too.

Let us begin our presentation of colour varieties with black (1), according to the established order. The occurrence of the black colour is determined by a dominant gene, which may often mask other colouring. To breed a quality Black Persian cat, perfect in its conformation and coat colour, is considered a real success among breeders.

3

Some Black Persian kittens display a rusty or grey coat until at least seven to eight months old. Only after the second moulting, at between 12 to 18 months of age, does the coat change its colour to deep black. When very young, single white hairs can appear in the coat. Both imperfections, however, tend to disappear with age and such kittens often have a much better coat when adult than cats showing pure black coats from the very beginning. We should always remember this when selecting animals for further breeding. A certain tendency

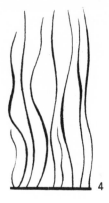

towards browning may be inherited from the parents, but will only be manifested in cats with a soft coat. White patches or a white chest are considered faults in kittens. This is because larger clusters of white hair are not liable to disappear, and will lead to the disqualification of a show cat. The tendency for deep orange eyes to turn green is another undesirable quality, which is much more frequent in Black Persians than in any other longhair variety.

White Longhair (White Persian)

White was one of the very first colours encountered in longhairs. According to the eye colour, White Persians were classed into several subgroups, which nowadays are recognized as separate breeds. These are Orange-eyed White Longhair (Copper-eyed White Persian) (2), Blue-eyed White Longhair (Blue-eyed White Persian) (3), and Odd-eyed White Longhair (Odd-eyed White Persian) (4) — having one eye blue and the other orange. Odd-eyed white cats actually have a very interesting look and this is perhaps why they are admired mainly by people who like curiosities. Blue-eyed whites are an old-established breed of cat. When the blue-eyed type was mated with male cats of other eye colours, the Orange-eyed White Longhair developed. Blue-eyed white cats are rarer than orange-eyed ones, as orange eye colour is much more easily inherited than blue. The blue eye colour of genuine Blue-eyed White Longhairs should be as deep as possible in order to be distinguished from the light blue eyes of semi-albinotic specimens. However, blue eyes are sometimes linked with deafness, as the gene for blue eye colour is frequently associated with the genes causing pathological changes in the inner ear.

White-coloured cats are not albinos, as laymen often believe. Their white colouring is caused by the dominant white gene. In spite of this fact, albino cats can occasionally occur. They are distinguished by a reddish eye colour. Since no pigment is laid down in their eyes, the red colour of the blood in the retinal vessels shows through clearly.

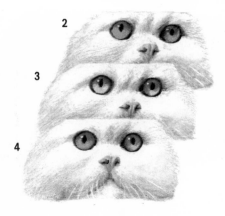

The White Longhair (1) must conform to the basic requirement of a snow-white coat. It is often achieved with difficulties, as the white coat frequently tends to turn yellow or at least acquires a yellowish tinge. The proper coat colour is passed on to the progeny. Improper colouring should be distinguished from a coat which has not been given sufficient grooming, since dead white hairs in the coat also create an impression of

1

yellowing. The same applies to dirty cats, which show a yellowish coat on different parts of their bodies.

It is not only pure white Persian kittens, but also shorthair breeds which frequently exhibit a dark-coloured or black smudge of irregular shape and size on the forehead or between the ears. The smudge disappears as the kitten becomes older.

Blue Longhair (Blue Persian)

Blue Persian cats (1) are very popular. Apart from the black, blue is one of the most common and among the oldest-known colourings. Queen Victoria is known to have kept a pair of Blue Persians. The Blue Persian has been recognized as a separate variety since 1898. All shades of blue or blue-grey are allowed for the coat. The true blue shades, such as lilac or a bright pastel blue, are considered to be first-rate, and are generally preferred by breeders. A blue shade which is too dark, or even a bluish-black colour, are regarded as less attractive. On the other hand, a darker coat colour is usually accompanied by a deeper orange or brown eye colour, which is considered a positive quality when assessing blue cats. Essential requirements for the coat colour include an overall even hue of the coat as well as self-coloured hairs throughout. Only around the tip of the nose is a slightly darker shade acceptable. Stripes, or any other ghost tabby pattern, are regarded as a serious fault in self-blue cats. If any pattern does occur, the animal is classed as a Blue Tabby Persian.

An overall darker hue, as well as dark markings on different parts of the body, can frequently be the result of large amounts of dead hair. In such cases, the cat needs a thorough grooming in order to remove the dead hair from the coat.

3

In Blue Persians, blue coat colour results from the presence of a dilute gene, which acts as a diluting agent, turning the basic black colour to blue. Another dilute gene operates in a similar way, reducing the intensity of the basic black and diluting it to chocolate (2). The black turns to lilac (3) in cases where both genes operate together. The above-mentioned varieties of Persians were originally obtained by experimental breeding. They have been recognized as separate breeds since 1983, so far remaining quite a rarity. Due to their attractive appearance, however, the have been much sought after by breeders especially the chocolate variety.

2

1

Red Self Longhair (Solid Red Persian)

Red Self Longhairs were recognized as a separate variety as early as the beginning of organized cat fancying, which was established in Britain around the year 1880. Their coat colour used to be orange rather than red and this is why the recent Red Self Persians (1, 2) used to be called Orange Persians before World War I. Red Self Persians were most widespread during the early 1930s. Superb specimens were known at that time, notably in Germany. During World War II, breeding of this colour variety declined. It took almost 20 years to re-establish the original level of the variety.

Nowadays, these rather attractively coloured cats are frequently ignored by breeders, for the following reasons. Firstly, it is considered a great success for the breeder to achieve a deep red coat colour of overall even hue and without any tabby stripes. Tabby markings persist notably on the face, legs and tail. Secondly, red tom cats frequently have a rather stocky conformation. This is probably the reason why they are selected for mating quite rarely, as breeders of Persian cats generally prefer more compact specimens to stocky ones.

Solid scarlet red or a deep mahogany shade are the most desirable coat colours in Red Self Persians. Apart from the tabby pattern, another imperfection is found in Red Self Persians. The self-coloured tail is sometimes white at the tip (3). In spite of careful selecting against such specimens, this defect is still rather difficult to remove.

1

2

A special method of improving the
quality and colour of the Red Self
Persian's coat is recommended by some
breeders for show preparation. Warm
bran should be rubbed into the coat and
then brushed out thoroughly. Just before
the show, a final gloss should be applied
with a piece of buff leather to give the
coat a gleaming appearance.

3

Cream Longhair (Cream Persian)

This variety is very popular due to its delicate and soft colour. The ancestors of most European Cream Persians (1) come from the United States, where this variety won the greatest popularity. Coat colours required by the standard nowadays are pastel cream or beige, deep ivory and buff-cream. At the beginning of the century, a cream colour with a ruddy shade used to be preferred. Nowadays, however, the ruddy colouring is no longer preferred. The main requirement is a pure and sound colouring without any darker stripes or markings. Originally, breeders used to select against animals with this defect. Since 1983, however, a special Cream Tabby Persian variety has been standardized.

A Cream Tabby Persian should have a distinct tabby pattern on its back, but this is encountered only rarely. When judging a cat, a lack of this feature is the most likely cause of penalties. Many Cream Persians have distinct tabby markings on their legs, but no pattern on the back. Cream coat colour genetically evolved from the orange by linkage with the dilute gene.

The large round eyes, coloured deep orange to copper, shine out against the pale cream coat, thus creating a superb overall impression. Cream cats are said to be quite shy.

2

Cream Tabby Persians remind many of Pallas's cats (the manul) (2), which is a wild member of the felids. According to one of the theories concerning the origin of the longhairs, the Persian cat descended from Pallas's cat. The manul is found in the high mountain regions of Asia. It has been discovered that in captivity Pallas's cats can interbreed with domestic cats. The manul resembles the Persian cat primarily because of its coat (which is quite long) and secondly by its flat skull with forward-facing eyes, as well as by the small rounded ears and short bushy tail.

1

Smoke Longhair (Black Smoke Persian)

Smoke Longhairs are among the most striking colour varieties due to the pensive, almost intelligent expression on their faces as well as their contrasting colouring. In a first-rate Smoke Longhair, the coloured head is surrounded by a dense silvery frill. The silvery undercoat is another feature characteristic of this variety. With the exception of the frill, flanks and tail, the undercoat cannot be seen on other parts of the body unless the cat is in motion. A walking smoke cat displays a silvery undercoat, which shows through on different parts of the body each time it moves. This makes the elegant cat's walk even more graceful. The well-developed ear tufts should be silvery as well. The Smoke Longhair has large round eyes, copper to deep orange in colour.

At present, eight colour varieties of smoke cats are known and recognized. The Smoke Longhair (Black Smoke Persian) (1) is the commonest variety. Blue Smoke Longhairs (see p. 42) can occasionally be seen at cat shows, while other varieties are very rare. These are Smoke Tortoiseshell (2), Smoke Chocolate Tortoiseshell, Smoke Lilac Tortoiseshell and Blue Cream Smoke (Smoke Dilute Tortoiseshell). Red Smoke and Cream Smoke cats, also called Red Cameo and Cream Cameo, are most common in Australia. The above mentioned varieties are rarely found in Europe.

1

2

A close look at an awn hair of a smoke
cat reveals that between a half and
two-thirds of the hair, from the tip
downwards, is pigmented (3); the rest of
the hair as well as the soft down hair is
silvery white, without any pigmentation.
This phenomenon is known as tipping. It
is determined by the presence of
a specific gene. Tipping occurs within
many colour varieties and breeds of cats.
In smokes, the tipping is very prominent,
while in cameos and chinchillas, which
are also bred in several colour varieties,
the pigmented part of the hair is much
smaller.

3

Blue Smoke Longhair (Blue Smoke Persian)

The blue-coloured variety of smoke cats (1) can sometimes be produced from Blue and Black Smoke matings. This is, however, exceptional, since the black is dominant over blue, thus usually masking the expression of the blue gene. Consequently, as a result of such crossing, Black Smokes are much more frequently born than Blue Smokes.

Smoke cats, which are a long-established variety, come under the general category of tipped longhairs. In 1860, smoke cats were described as a specific coat colour. No genetic laws were known at the time and therefore they were considered to be a result of chance mating of Black, Blue and White Longhairs. They used to be very popular, especially in Britain. The world's first list of male cats kept for breeding was drawn up there as early as 1912. It included 18 smoke specimens. During World War II, the breeding of Persians on the Continent dwindled. In Britain, the interest in smoke cats was naturally reduced to a minimum as well. The present level of breeding was achieved only in the 1950s, owing primarily to the import of smokes from across the Atlantic.

However, breeders of smoke cats are at a disadvantage, as these animals are usually in top show condition only for a short period of the year. This period usually occurs later than in other longhair varieties, because they have a prolonged period of moulting. During this period, tabby markings can appear on many parts of the body. In addition, the frill — one of the most typical features — is usually shed, too.

2

1

Kittens of smoke cats (2) have a rather atypical colouring at birth, and therefore it is quite difficult to determine whether or not they are a real smoke variety. The kittens are often born almost entirely black, blue or otherwise coloured. A specific silver tracing around the eyes and under the nose, known as 'clown lines', is a typical distinguishing feature, according to which the kittens can be classed as smokes. However, it can be observed only for a short period after the birth, as it disappears within a few days.

The rest of the undercoat is of the same shade as the outer colouring. The silvery hairs do not begin to show until the kittens are about two to three weeks old. The number of silvery hairs also gradually increases. Thus, a six to eight week old kitten looks like a perfect spotted specimen, being by no means reminiscent of a smoke cat. The silvery frill appears as late as three or four months of age. The true appearance of the typical smoke-coloured cat does not emerge until the sixth month, however.

Shell Cameo

Persian cats with red tipping, in other words with red-coloured ends of the hairs, first appeared in the United States around the year 1934, as a result of uncontrolled matings between self reds and chinchillas. In order to preserve their own special charm, the planned breeding of cameos began around the year 1950. In the United States, they have been standardized and recognized as a breed since 1960. In Europe, the first cameos appeared after 1955. They were recognized as a breed only in 1975.

As the cameos are reminiscent of chinchillas due to the red (1) or cream tipping, they were originally called Red Chinchillas. From the genetic point of view, however, the nature of their colouring is different from chinchillas, and therefore, when categorizing the breeds and colour varieties, the cameos are considered as related to the smoke cats. Consequently, any breeding combination of cameos and chinchillas is undesirable. Kittens born from such matings are registered in experimental stock books only. Apart from the atypical coloration, these specimens often have green eyes like those of chinchillas, while the eyes of cameos should be deep orange or copper.

Cameos are reminiscent of chinchillas in respect of another, very attractive trait. Their eye rims, nose and paw pads are a conspicuous pink colour. Only in tortoiseshell varieties does the colour of these parts correspond to the basic piebald colouring with the prevalence of black, blue, chocolate (chestnut) or lilac.

The presence of the tipped hairs on the mask (2), legs and upperside of the tail is the basic trait of cameos. Pure white hairs must be present in the undercoat, on the chin, in tufts of hairs projecting from the ears, on the frill, chest, belly and underside of the tail. These parts of the body should not show any tipped hair.

According to both European and American standards, the undercoat should be ivory white, while the British standard allows off-white to a very light cream undercoat. In tortoiseshell varieties, the white colour should have a silvery shade.

2

1

Shaded Cameo

Current show standards have so far recognized a total number of 12 varieties of cameos, corresponding to the character of the overall coat colour and tipped colours. According to the degree of tipping, however, cameos can be classed into two basic groups. These are the Shell Cameo (see the previous two pages) with the hair tipped only to one-eight of its length (3) and the Shaded Cameo (1) with the hair tipped to approximately one-third of its length (4), thus being more heavily pigmented than Shell Cameos. Within these two groups cameos are then distinguished by the colour of the tipping. These are the colour varieties recognized by European standards: Red Cameo, Cream Cameo, Tortoiseshell Cameo, Blue-Cream Cameo (Dilute Tortoise-shell Cameo), Chocolate Tortoiseshell Cameo and Lilac Tortoiseshell Cameo. In addition to the varieties mentioned, the Tabby Cameo has been recognized recently.

Red Cameos and Cream Cameos, with rose-coloured paw pads (2), are the most frequently encountered varieties. Cameos with other coat colours are very rare. It is rather difficult to distinguish between the colours, especially in the shell group.

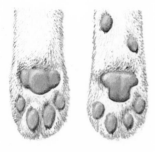

2

If more than just the terminal half of the hair is coloured, the variety is called Red or Cream Smoke (Smoke Cameo) (5). Hairs of such cats are tipped from a half to two-thirds of their length (see Blue Smoke Longhair on page 42).

It is not possible to distinguish the new-born kittens of cameo varieties from pure white ones. They begin to acquire the proper coat at about two weeks of age. By this time, separate tipped hairs begin to appear on the white undercoat, especially on the face.

1

3　4

5

Silver Tabby Longhair (Silver Tabby Persian)

The Silver Tabby variety (1) belongs to the very oldest known colour variety of Persians. It used to be very popular, but has been produced much less frequently by breeders recently. The main reason is probably the recent popularity of characteristic very short, almost stunted noses, such as are found in the Peke-faced Persian. Although a short nose is typical of the Persians, the nose length of all tabby varieties is close to the upper limit. This applies to the body conformation as well. Unfortunately, it is quite difficult to breed a tabby cat with a good head type (2) as well as with a perfect ebony black tabby pattern and a typical eye colour. Such an ideal combination of all three basic requirements for the animal's appearance seldom occurs.

The origin of the word 'tabby' is most likely derived from *Attabiah*, which is the name of the district in Baghdad from where many animals with a typical tabby pattern used to be exported, especially to Britain and France.

Breeding of Silver Tabbies with other longhair varieties is of rather limited value. Although some combinations could probably produce positive elements, for instance the above-mentioned peke-faced type with a shorter nose, such a combination can either suppress the characteristic tabby pattern, or it can lead to a loss of the typical green colour, which is a result of mating with an orange-eyed male.

The eyes of Silver Tabbies should be green to orange or hazel, having the shade of unripe hazel nuts. Although the hazel shade is accepted, it is not the most desirable colour. The eyes should be rimmed with black, as in the chinchillas. The nose colour is also the same as in chinchillas. It should be brick red and black-rimmed.

The Silver Tabby Longhair variety can be found in four colour variations. They differ in the colour of the dark pattern on the ground colour, which is silver-tipped. It is the silvery ground colour that distinguishes the Silver Tabby from other tabby varieties. The Blue Silver Tabby has a blue-coloured pattern. Other variations are Chocolate Silver Tabby and Lilac Silver Tabby, bearing chocolate or lilac patterns.

2

1

Brown Tabby Longhair (Brown Tabby Persian)

Except for the Silver Tabby, which has a tipped coat (see the previous two pages), the coats of all tabby varieties have ticking developed on each hair. Ticking is determined by a specific gene, also known as the agouti-factor. The action of the agouti-factor results in an alternating pigmentation of varying intensity in each hair. This means that each hair with ticking has a characteristic distinct banding.

Like the above-mentioned Silver Tabby and other tabbies, the Brown Tabby Longhair (1, 2) should have exact and contrasting markings, which create their peculiar characteristic appearance. The underlying coat of Brown Tabbies has a warm, golden brown shade with a gentle buff undertone. It bears a clear and distinct black pattern. The underlying coat grows darker with age. The eyes are copper or deep orange. The eyelids are rimmed with black. The muzzle is brick red and black-rimmed.

Among ticked longhair tabbies, other varieties are recognized and justly admired. These are Blue Tabby, Chocolate Tabby, Lilac Tabby, Red Tabby and Cream Tabby. They differ not only in the colour of the pattern, but also in the representation of ticked colours in the underlying coat.

Brown Tabby Longhairs used to be much more popular than they are today. Their breeding accelerated especially towards the end of the last century. This was, however, quite a different type of cat from the present Persian. In fact, they were simply domestic cats with a long coat. Although the name Brown Tabby is recognized by the standard, genetically it is properly termed Black or Ebony Tabby.

Kittens of all tabby varieties are born almost self-coloured. The stripes are barely visible on the legs and sides. The tabby pattern only becomes fully developed at four or six months of age. When selecting a kitten for further breeding, one should stick to the following rule: the darker the new-born kitten, the better the colouring it will have

1

2

at maturity. If tabby kittens are born with a distinct pattern such as that of mature animals, the coat will turn pale and the pattern will become blurred after six months at the latest. Such animals are no longer suitable for breeding.

Blue Tabby Longhair (Blue Tabby Persian)

Blue Tabby Longhairs (1) are perhaps the most attractive and the most graceful of tabby varieties. This is due to the considerable contrast between the ground coat colour and the pattern it bears. The ivory colour with pale blue ticking has deep blue markings. In Blue Tabby Longhairs, only the blotched 'classic' pattern occurs. So far, no striped (mackerel) Blue Tabby Longhairs have been bred. Apart from the attractively coloured coat, the Blue Tabby has brilliant deep orange to copper eyes, which are rimmed with deep blue on the eyelids. The muzzle should be an 'old-rose' colour with a deep blue rim as well. The paw pads should be greyish-blue. This colour variety has appeared only recently. It was only recognized by cat fanciers' associations in the United States as recently as 1962, and as late as 1977 by the FIFe, the European cat fanciers' organization.

Persian tabbies usually show two or three spiral lines on the cheeks near the outer eye corners. Since these resemble a pair of spectacles, the pattern is sometimes called after this effect. On the forehead, there are several vertical stripes, which are arranged into the shape of an 'M'. Due to the pattern on the face, the animals look as if they are smiling. Between the eyes, there are several lines running down to the nose; the stripes run across the head down to the neck and then along the spine. In the middle of the spine there are usually three parallel stripes, from which further, thinner stripes run down the sides. The distance between the stripes should be as wide as the stripes themselves. This is known as the striped or mackerel tabby pattern (2). Another pattern is called the blotched ('classic') or standard tabby pattern (3).

There is a circular pattern on the
shoulders, and an oval oyster-shaped
whorl appears on the flanks. The overall
pattern resembles a butterfly wing. The
forelegs and hindlegs are cross-banded
almost all over. On the chest, there are
wider, unbroken stripes in the shape of
necklaces, known as 'mayoral chains'.
They also appear on the neck and on the
sides they run as far as the spine line and
to the edge of the butterfly pattern. The
tail should be regularly striped, with
a dark tip. On the stomach, spotting is
laid on the ground colour. Preferably,
the spots should not merge.

3   2

1

Red Tabby Longhair (Red Tabby Persian)

The Red Tabby Longhair (1) is today one of the most widely bred of the longhair tabby varieties. It should have a distinct, deep rich red to mahogany pattern on a pale red background, with ticking. Thus, it is the contrast between the two tones of red, which is the decisive factor in Red Tabbies. This is substantially different from Brown and Blue Tabbies, in which the contrast is created by two different colours and not merely by varying intensity of shading of a single colour. The same applies to the rarer cream variety. Here, the difference is only in the intensity of cream colour. Unfortunately, Red or Cream Tabbies often have an indistinct or even blurred pattern, be it mackerel or standard. At the show, it is sometimes difficult to judge the animal in its proper colour class, as it doesn't correspond to the standard requirements for either Red Tabbies or Red Selfs (see page 36). In addition, the problem is further complicated by the fact that at certain times of the year moulting also occurs. Thus the same cat can have the appearance of a Red Tabby during one particular season of the year, while at other times it resembles a Red Self variety. The main feature principally distinguishing the two varieties is the presence of ticking in the Red Tabby Longhair; there is no ticking in the hair of the Red Self. Before this genetic difference was discovered, both varieties used to be judged in a single category. In the Red Tabby Longhair, as in the Red Self, any white markings are considered to be a fault (2). They may appear on the chin, chest or on the tip of the tail, and are penalized at shows.

1

2

A special method is used when preparing the coat of all tabby Persians for the show. Almost all colour varieties of longhairs and semi-longhairs have a distinct, longer coat on the neck, known as the frill. It should be groomed out from the body to accentuate the head. In those tabby varieties in which the perfect tabby pattern should be emphasized, the frill should be groomed in the direction of the grain. No grooming powder should be used on tabby Persians, although it is often recommended for other varieties, especially those with paler shades. The tabby markings should have as great a contrast as possible. The powder applied to the coat may blur the desirable contrasts.

Chinchilla (Silver Persian)

The name of this most impressive colour variety is derived from the small South American rodent, the fur of which was prized by the ancient Incas. Nowadays, chinchillas are bred on farms, and are rare in the wild. Rabbit breeders have also developed a 'chinchilla' breed, the fur of which is reminiscent of that of the original rodent. The first longhaired chinchilla cats appeared in the 1880s in England. They were the result of matings between silver tabbies and smokes.

Guard and awn hairs with distinct tipping are the basic features of the chinchilla (1). Each hair is black-tipped to at most one-eighth of its length (3). Tipped hairs should appear only on the back, sides, head, ears and upperside of the tail. Other parts of the body, ear tufts included, should remain pure white and without tipping. In addition to standard chinchillas, blue, chocolate and lilac varieties have recently been bred. Apart from the attractive sparkling coat, the superb impression created by chinchillas is highlighted by the eyeliner effect around the expressive eyes (2), which are emerald or blue-green in colour. In the basic silver variety, the eyes are rimmed with black or dark brown, while in other varieties the rims can be blue, brown or lavender-pink, in harmony with the ground colour. The brick red muzzle should be rimmed as well. The colour of the paw pads should be the same as that of the rims.

Silver Persians, or Chinchillas, appeared about 100 years ago. Over the course of this century, certain changes in their appearance have occurred. Early chinchillas used to be much darker than those found nowadays . They had more pigmented hair and the tipping was rather heavy, just like in the present Silver Shaded Persian. Thus, the early standard chinchillas exhibited quite a distinct tabby pattern. Their legs were much shorter and, in general, they were smaller and more dainty looking than the recent chinchillas. The long legs of the chinchillas bred nowadays are probably a consequence of insufficient selection and repeated mating to males of the same variety. Mating to males of other varieties has a rather unfavourable effect on the coat and eye colour. Unfortunately, the most typical features of chinchillas, the silvery tipped coat and green eyes, are suppressed by mating with the rest of the Persian varieties. Shaded Silver Persian males can be used but when mating chinchillas to Silver Tabby Longhairs, breeders usually run the risk of producing partially marked kittens.

2

3

1

Silver Shaded Persian

Silver Shaded Persians (in Britain termed pewters) (1) were not standardized until 1976, although they had been known for more than 70 years. In Britain, they were distinguished from Chinchillas as early as 1902. In spite of this fact, they were described either as 'darker chinchillas', or they were considered to be one of the unrecognized Persian breeds. In fact, the greater degree of silver tipping is the only feature that distinguishes them from Chinchillas. Each awn hair (3) should be tipped to a maximum of one-third of its length. Tipping should only be found on the mantle (the back, sides, head and upperside of the tail). No tipping should be found on the snow-white chin, chest and underside of the tail. The Chinchilla creates an overall impression of a silvery white cat, while the Silver Shaded Persian has a sort of icy zinc tint. The eye colour is as for the Chinchilla — green or turquoise. The colour varieties of Silver Shaded Persians are the same as for Chinchillas: the standard black, blue, chocolate and lilac. The eye rims, the visible skin which rims the brick red muzzle as well as the colour of the paw pads should match the overall tone.

Golden Chinchillas (2), of which there are two varieties — Shell and Shaded — are classed with silver Chinchillas and Silver Shaded Persians. Tipped hair is found on the same parts of the body. Requirements for the eye colour, the colour of the nose tip and paw pads are also the same. The only difference is found in the ground colour of the coat. In Golden Chinchillas, it is mid apricot to warm reddish-brown. The blackish tipping thus gives a sparkling golden appearance. Golden Chinchillas represent one of the most recent varieties of the breed. They were recognized in Europe only in 1983.

In Chinchillas and Silver Shaded
Persians, the kittens of all colour varieties
are much darker in colour than mature
animals. They look like Brown Tabby
Longhair kittens. They may have tabby
markings all over the body, or only on the
back and tail. Their coat is usually much
shorter than that of other Persians.
Tipped hairs begin to show through the
coat after about four to six weeks.
Similarly, the eye colour becomes
partially established by the age of six
months; the proper colour appears as late
as about two years of age.

As chinchillas have a rather delicate
skin, one should be very careful when
grooming their coats. It is not
recommended to trim their coat for the
summer, as is often the practice with
other Persians. This is because it takes
quite a long time for perfect tipping to
develop.

2

3

1

Bicoloured Black-and-white Longhair (Parti-coloured Persian)

Let us begin our presentation of bicoloured longhairs with the black-and-white colour variety (1). A great number of bicolours (originally known as magpie cats) appeared as a result of almost all breeding experiments. They were also found in litters of tortoiseshells and blue creams. However, they were given recognition only after many years of breeding. In Britain, they were recognized by the GCCF in 1966. In Europe, they were accepted by the FIFe in 1969 and in the United States, the CFA recognized the parti-colours as late as 1971. In spite of the official recognition, breeders of bicolours had difficulties, as the original show standard required a bicolour to be marked exactly the same as the Dutch rabbit. Dutch rabbits should have clearly defined and well-broken patches around the ears. The large patch of colour on the back and the patches on the head should not run together. It is quite easy to meet this strict requirement with rabbits. The rabbit which is not acceptable by the standard can simply be removed from the breeding programme. But what was to be done with kittens which were not up to the standard, though otherwise perfect in all respects? Several cat fancy organizations raised their voices against the strict standard and two years later, in 1971, the standard was amended and some flexibility of pattern was allowed.

3

Nowadays, bicolours need only have a balanced ratio of both colours, white and the other recognized self-colour. In a perfect specimen, not more than two-thirds of the coat should be coloured and not more than half should be white. The colour should be pure, without any stripes or markings. The colours are to make clearly defined and well-composed patches (3). In practice this means that both colours should be present on the face, legs and possibly on the tail. Bicolours usually have a white streak or

2

patch between the coloured parts of the
face. This is known as the blaze (2).
Though not obligatory, the blaze is
considered a positive quality when
assessing a bicoloured specimen
at a show.

1

Bicoloured Blue-and-white Longhair (Parti-coloured Persian)

The Bicoloured Blue-and-white Longhair is a colour variety of long-hairs which can be bred from the black-and-white (see page 60) variety (picture 1 shows the Angora, not the Persian type). Although the blue colour is not as intense as the black, this colour combination is rather impressive and therefore popular. The requirements for the distribution of blue and white colour throughout the animal's coat are the same as for the other bicolours. The eye colour of bicolours is subject to equally strict requirements. The eyes should be deep orange or copper. The muzzle and paw pads are pink, thus corresponding to the white coat colour. It follows that their colouring may match any of the colour variants.

Blue-and-white Longhairs are one of the basic bicoloured varieties used for breeding tricoloured cats.

The following colour varieties of bicoloured longhairs are recognized by current standards: Black-and-white, Blue-and-white, Red-and-white, Cream-and-white, Chocolate-and-white and Lilac-and-white. All varieties are quite common worldwide, except for the last two, which so far remain rarities.

2

Bicolours which do not correspond to the standard requirements as regards the colour proportions are to be found quite frequently. They usually occur in litters resulting from the matings of bicoloured males to bicoloured females. In extreme cases, their progeny may be almost pure white, exhibiting only small patches of colour on some parts of the body. The colour is restricted to one-sixth of the cat's coat. These cats resemble the semi-longhair Turkish breed in coat colour. This distinct variant of bicolours is known as Van-pattern Persians (2) in the United States. They are assessed in a special class separate from standard bicolours. From 1986, these cats were recognized as a separate group called Harlequins by cat fanciers' associations affiliated with the FIFe. The whole underside of the body should be pure white. The eyes should be coloured the same as in White Longhairs — in other words orange, blue or odd (one eye blue, the other orange). These specimens are rather valuable for further breeding, as appropriate mating results in offspring with superb bicoloured coats.

1

Bicoloured Red-and-white Longhair (Parti-coloured Persian)

The following two varieties of bicolours are also rather widespread: Red-and-white Longhair (1) and Cream-and-white Longhair (2). The latter could be, and in fact was, produced from the former, as cream results from the genetic action of the dilute gene on the orange. In both varieties, the coloured part of the coat shows distinct bands or shading rather frequently. This is regarded as a considerable depreciation of the animal's breeding qualities. The gene determining red or cream coat colour is frequently linked with the predisposition for tabby pattern. Where the pattern is not very distinct, it is usually tolerated when assessing the cats at shows.

According to the standard, the eyes of Red-and-white Longhairs and Cream-and-white Longhairs should be deep orange to copper. As it generally corresponds to the coat colour, breeders of these varieties usually have no difficulties with eye colour.

3

Short-nosed animals appeared as a result of breeding experiments. They are found above all in longhairs which show red or cream coat colour. As they resemble the Pekinese dog, these cats are known as Peke-faced Persians (3). The bridge of the nose is flat and it appears depressed between the eyes. The high forehead bulges over the nose to form a sharp stop. The nose is almost invisible in profile, being hidden by massive vaulted cheeks. In addition, Peke-faced Persians exhibit a characteristic fold of skin running from the bridge of the nose to the outer edges of the cheeks. From the anatomical point of view, this is regarded as a deformation.

As a consequence of the considerably shorter nose, deformations of nasal bones and upper jaw occur. Therefore, Peke-faced Persians are often prone to running eyes due to blockages of the tear ducts. They can also show an undershot jaw. This means that the normal lower jaw and the shortened upper jaw do not meet correctly.

2

1

Tortoiseshell Longhair (Tortoiseshell Persian)

The first Tortoiseshell Longhairs (1) appeared in shows as early as 1900, and have been popular and widely bred ever since. The most interesting feature of tortoiseshells is the variation of colouring. Many breeders are also attracted by the fact that the kittens usually exhibit a diversity of colours. This is because the tortoiseshell colouring is genetically determined by the female sex. Tortoiseshells should therefore be mated to males of other colours. For example, after the Tortoiseshell female was mated to a Red Self male, Black males, Red Self males and females as well as Tortoiseshell females can appear in the litter. Males showing a tabby pattern or ticking are not recommended for mating, as kittens of non-standard colours can appear in the litter.

The tortoiseshell colours prescribed by the standard are different shades of red and black. Originally, three colours were mentioned: black, red and cream. The pattern should be even and well-proportioned, and well-broken into patches which should be bright and rich in colour. It is rather attractive as well as desirable for the colours to be well broken on the face, thus dividing it into two halves — dark and light. A cream or red blaze on the dark part or in the middle of the forehead is especially favoured. The ears and legs should be variably patched as well, both colours being well-broken into discrete patches. Faint stripes on the coat can sometimes be tolerated (they indicate that the animal has a tabby ancestor). However, distinct tabby markings as well as the presence of a great number of white or ticked hairs are penalized by judges.

As regards the distribution of colour patches, European standards differ from those in North America, as the latter require considerably larger areas of uniform colour than the former.

In kittens of Tortoiseshell Longhairs, the difference between red and cream colour is quite indistinct. The colours become brighter and red hairs appear only after the period of moulting, which occurs between four and six months, and sometimes even later. The future black colouring begins as a dirty blue shade.

As the result of appropriate genetic action, the black colour may be reduced in intensity. Consequently, apart from the standard black colouring, chocolate and lilac varieties can be found, in addition to the blue variety which results from the presence of another gene. All varieties mentioned so far remain rather rare. The Blue Cream (Dilute) Tortoiseshell has not yet been recognized as a separate breed.

Tortoiseshell-and-white Longhair (Calico Persian)

A very interesting colouring can sometimes be obtained from mating Black, Blue, Red or Cream Tortoiseshell and Blue Cream females to Bicoloured Longhair males. These cats are known as Tortoiseshell-and-white Longhairs, or Tortie-and-white Longhairs in Britain and Calico Persians in the United States (1, 2). They used to be termed chintz cats as well. In fact, calico cats are tortoiseshells with white patches added. Just like the predominant colours, white patches should be clearly defined and well distributed. Not more than two-thirds of the cat's coat should be coloured and not more than half should be white. The American standard makes a good summary of the required characteristics: 'the Tortoiseshell-and-white pattern should resemble a tortoiseshell cat that has been dropped in a pail of milk.' In the United States, this variety was recognized as late as 1956. The white patches are desirable on the back, stomach, legs and chest and at least a small amount of white should be found on the face, resembling a blaze. On the whole, white patches can be found on any part of the body as long as the desired proportion to other colours (black, red or cream) is preserved. Crossing of tortoiseshell-and-white females is controlled by the same laws as for bicolours: mating to the bicoloured male can result in Van-patterned, or Harlequin, progeny.

Just like tortoiseshells, calicoes are always females. Once seldom seen at shows, calicoes are very popular and much sought after nowadays. In Japan, they are believed to bring luck. Presenting somebody with a calico cat is considered a great favour.

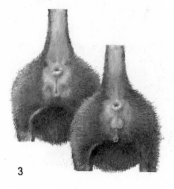

3

Novices often ask how to determine the sex of new-born kittens. It is quite easy with Tortoiseshell, Tortie-and-white or Blue Cream Longhairs, as these are always female varieties. In the case of other Persian kittens, the sex is best determined one to two days after birth (3). Females have a slit vulva, almost joined to the anus in the shape of an exclamation mark (!) when viewed from below and from behind. In males, genital and anal openings are round and much more separated, thus resembling a semicolon (:). Also, two raised areas

2

can be seen between the openings. These
are the scrotal sacs for the testicles, which
have not yet descended. A kitten cannot
be sexed by the size of its head;
a difference between a large and more
delicate head is only typical of adult
animals.

1

Blue Cream and White Tortoiseshell Longhair
(Dilute Calico)

The Blue Cream and White Tortoiseshell Longhair (1, 2) is derived from the Tortie-and-white Longhair. By incorporating the dilute gene, the black and red colours are reduced in intensity. Consequently, apart from the white patches, these cats exhibit blue and cream patches as well. They come under the general category of tricoloured cats, or tricolours. In the United States, the variety is described as the Dilute Calico. The tricoloured cat is rather impressive, having a delicate fluffy appearance. No male tricolours occur, just as in other combinations with red and cream. Although Dilute Calicoes received recognition as a separate breed and are much sought after by breeders, they occur rather rarely on the whole. This is because their occurrence is determined by deliberate mating. For example, to obtain a tricoloured cat, self females must be mated to bicoloured males, preferably blue-and-white or cream-and-white. And vice versa, bicoloured, calico or tricoloured females should be crossed with self males. However, apart from the bicoloured and self kittens of both sexes, tortoiseshell or tortie-and-white kittens are more likely to appear in the litter than blue cream and white tortoiseshells.

The dilute gene b operates in a similar way, diluting the black to chocolate. When the genes b and d act in co-operation, the chocolate colour turns to lilac. Consequently, other derived varieties are the Chocolate Tortoiseshell and White Longhair (Chestnut Calico) and the Lilac Cream and White Longhair (Lavender Calico). Despite occurring only rarely, both varieties have show standards.

In the Blue Cream and White Tortoiseshell Longhair, standard requirements for the distribution of the three basic colours correspond to those for the Tortoiseshell-and-white. This means that all three colours should be of a bright shade, well distributed and well broken into patches. The muzzle and paw pads should be grey-blue or pink, or grey-blue spotted with pink. In chocolate and lilac varieties, they should be coloured milk chocolate or lilac.

2

1

Blue Cream Longhair (Blue Cream Persian)

Tortoiseshells gave rise to another, no less attractive colour variety, which is known as the Blue Cream Longhair (1). By the presence of the appropriate gene, the original black is changed to blue and the red to cream. In contrast with the tortoiseshell pattern, both colours should be evenly intermingled, giving an effect rather like a colour mix. Clearly defined patches of either colour are considered a fault. This is the principal difference between the Blue Cream and the Tortoiseshell Longhairs. The blaze desirable on the forehead of Tortoise-shell Longhairs would also be considered an imperfection in Blue Cream Longhairs.

Blue Cream Longhairs have been common in Europe since the 1920s, when they were exhibited in Britain for the first time. They were recognized as a separate colour variety in 1930. Nowadays they are among the most popular and attractive of varieties. As with Tortoiseshell Longhairs, Blue Creams are almost always female. Although there are cases of male Blue Creams recorded in the specialized literature, these specimens died soon after birth or proved to be sterile.

The mingled pattern of colours was only required by European standards. On the American continent there are quite different requirements for the coloration of Blue Cream Persians. The American Blue Cream Persian (2) is, in fact, a Blue Persian with clear cream patches on the body, tail, legs and face. The cream blaze on the face is particularly desirable.

Blue Cream kittens are born almost self blue, with only mere faint hints of the future cream fur. During the course of development the amount of cream hair increases, thus creating the desirable streaks of colour.

Blue Cream Longhairs are obtained by mating a Cream female to a Blue male or a Blue female to a Cream male. Blue male kittens in the litter result from mating to a Cream male while Creams are produced from mating to a Blue male.

When preparing Blue Cream Longhairs for the show, a powder should always be used, but should be brushed out thoroughly. The powder makes the coat look softer, reducing the possible contrasts between the colours.

1

2

Seal Colourpoint (Seal Point Himalayan)

Breeders have always attempted to establish a cat with Persian coat, conformation and head type, which at the same time exhibits the pigmented points and deep blue eyes which are found in the Siamese and some other breeds. The heavily pigmented points occur on the face, ears, feet and paws as well as on the tail. They give the cat a very special, almost demoniac charm, which reminds many of wild feline species. A variety of point colours exists, and therefore, Colourpoint Longhairs are found in a number of colour varieties. In the United States, the breed is known as the Himalayan, as it resembles the Himalayan rabbit in colour.

The contrast between the coat and point colours is the essential as well as the most attractive feature of Colourpoint Longhairs. The Seal Colourpoint (1, 2) shows the most dramatic contrast of all. There is a distinct contrast between the cream body colour of the coat and the dark brown or reddish-brown points. Dark brown points are known to cat fanciers as seal, and hence the name of the variety. The muzzle and paw pads of this variety should be dark brown in keeping with the points colour.

The cream-coloured coat may lose its original shade, turning darker. This is a regular phenomenon, which occurs quite frequently, especially in elderly cats. In young cats, however, a darkish coat is considered a fault. Such cats would be too dark when adult. This is regarded as a fault at shows, as the characteristic contrast becomes dimmed. Contrary to the rest of Colourpoint Longhairs, elderly Blue Colourpoints (see page 76) may show a darker coat as well.

1

2

Blue Colourpoint (Blue Point Himalayan)

Random matings produced longhaired specimens with Siamese points in litters of Siamese cats as early as 1920, for example in Sweden. These cats did not, however, give rise to Colourpoint Longhairs, which are the result of a deliberate crossing between Persian and Siamese cats. In 1930, two Americans, Clyde Keeler and Virginia Cobb, attempted to produce a truly Persian cat with the Siamese colouring, this time under more scientific conditions. Later, British breeders shared their interest in breeding. The experiments were interrupted by World War II, and thus it was not until the end of the 1940s that true Colourpoint Longhairs, such as those known today, were created. In 1955, Colourpoint Longhairs were recognized as a separate breed in Britain and on the Continent. In 1957 the breed was given recognition in America, where it is most widely bred.

    Colourpoint Longhairs are of the same body type as other Persians. The body should be short and cobby. Yet specimens exhibiting a distincly elongated body are found quite frequently. This is the manifestation of the original features typical of the Siamese, which was one of the breeds involved in establishing the Colourpoint.

Just like regular longhairs, the Blue Colourpoint (1, 2) results from the action of the dilute gene on the basic black colour. In Colourpoints, the basic colour is dark brown. Thus, dark brown points are diluted to blue. Blue points should tone in with the glacial blue to lilac body colour of the coat. Unfortunately, this colour frequently acquires a deeper blue tinge, thus dimming the desirable contrasts. The muzzle and paw pads should be slate blue, in keeping with the coat and points colour. Blue Colourpoints usually have very attractive eyes, matching the overall colouring.

76

2

1

Chocolate Colourpoint (Chocolate Point Himalayan)

As already mentioned, the body type and soft voice of Persians combined with the typical blue eyes and Siamese-type points constitute the characteristic features of all Colourpoint colour varieties. It is rather difficult for breeders to succeed in maintaining all the desirable features in the Colourpoint breed, however. As Colourpoints were produced only recently, the heredity of traits has not yet been fully 'encoded'. Thus it frequently happens that one of the desirable traits does not show itself. It is very hard for the breeder to re-establish the particular lost trait in his breed.

This applies particularly to the blue eyes and short nose of the Persian type. Unfortunately, the two are seldom found together. The breeder focusing on producing blue eyes usually fails to preserve the desired short nose. Thus his animals may have noses which are very Siamese-like in shape. Alternatively, a perfect short nose is usually accompanied by light blue eyes. Nevertheless, the two traits mentioned are most desirable in Colourpoints, being regarded as hallmarks of the breed. The breeder must show great perseverance, carefully selecting the animals suitable for further breeding.

2

1

Chocolate Colourpoints as well as Lilac (Frost) Colourpoints may be produced by incorporating the dilute genes which reduce black to chocolate and chocolate to lilac. The body colour of the Chocolate Colourpoint (1,2) should be ivory, with chocolate-coloured points. The muzzle should be milk chocolate, the paw pads cinnamon to chocolate. The Lilac Colourpoint should have a magnolia body colour with lilac points, the muzzle and paw pads should be pink.

Red Colourpoint (Red Point Himalayan)

The Red Colourpoint (1) is among the most attractive of varieties. Although a few specimens had been bred earlier, the variety has only been widely known since the mid-1970s. As with reds of other breeds, the red colour of the points is usually accompanied by the 'classic' or mackerel tabby pattern of variable visibility. Tabby markings most frequently appear on the forehead and front legs. A uniform red shade without any tabby markings occurs rather rarely, as the orange gene is usually linked with the gene determining the tabby pattern.

A similar variety was developed on the American continent. The points are deep red, almost orange-purple. The variety is known as the Flame Point Himalayan (2), being free of any hints of tabby markings at the points. As the Flame Point Himalayan does not occur in Europe, it is not recognized by the FIFe.

1

2

The indistinct contrast between the body colour and the colouring at the points is the most frequent fault encountered by breeders of Colourpoints. The coat colour as well as the colour at the points is frequently dispersed, bearing traces of tabby markings (see page 87). The coloured mask on the face is sometimes separated from the ear points. Occasionally it may reach too far, running down to the back as well.

A distinct dark patch on the underparts is another imperfection, which was transferred from the Siamese to Colourpoints. The deformation of the caudal vertebrae known as the kink is another imperfection inherited from the Siamese ancestors. The kink used to be quite common but, fortunately, is found only rarely nowadays.

Cream Colourpoint (Cream Point Himalayan)

The Cream Colourpoint (1) differs from the Red Colourpoint only in the shade of points colour. It is therefore rather difficult to tell them apart only by the points. In addition, both varieties exhibit the same colour on the paw pads and muzzle. The points of the Red Colourpoint should be a warm orange shade, while those of the Cream Colourpoint are pastel cream. The body of the coat should be a magnolia white colour with a cream tinge, while the Cream Colourpoint should be coloured bright cream-white. Considering the fact that over the course of the year most cats show minor departures from their normal coat colour — which are dependent on the degree of moulting and the growth rate of the new coat — it is actually extremely difficult to determine the colour variety properly.

Colourpoint kittens (2) of all varieties are born without points. They are of uniform pale colour, showing only a hint of the future body colouring. This applies to the other breeds with coloured points too. The points colour does not begin to appear until the sixth week of age. Until this time, kittens can only be distinguished by the colour of the muzzle and paw pads although at birth this is not very distinct either. Colourpoint kittens can be distinguished from the adult animals by the fluffy hair between the ears.

2

1

Tortie Colourpoint (Tortie Himalayan)

As with Persians with fully coloured coats, Tortie Colourpoints are classified according to the basic shade of the points. They are divided into four varieties: Seal Tortie Colourpoint, Blue Tortie Colourpoint (1), Chocolate Tortie Colourpoint and Lilac Tortie Colourpoint. Accordingly, points colours are brown, blue, chocolate and lilac, sometimes mixed with patches of red (in Seal Tortie Colourpoint) or cream (in the rest of the varieties). The patches should be well broken. In the main, this is the basic requirement for the tortoiseshell colouring. The muzzle and paw pads of the Seal Tortie Colourpoint should be seal, pink or pink patched with seal. In the Blue Tortie Colourpoint (2), they should be grey-blue, pink or grey-blue patched with pink. The muzzle and paw pads of the chocolate variety should be chocolate, pink or a combination of the two. Similarly, the Lilac Tortie Colourpoint has the muzzle and paw pads coloured in lilac, pink or pink with lilac patches.

Let us say a few words about the temperament of Colourpoints. Experienced breeders claim these cats to be rather active, but less so than Siamese. Nor are they as noisy as Siamese. They are extremely self-conscious, almost proud. On the other hand, their exceptional attachment to man should be stressed as well. They usually enjoy being stroked. As with Persians, litters normally contain three or four kittens. Colourpoints usually rear their young with great care. They mature as early as eight months — somewhat earlier than is the case with other Persians.

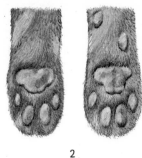

2

1

Tabby (Lynx) Colourpoint (Tabby Point Himalayan)

Depending on the body colour and points colour on the face, ears, legs, paws and tail, Colourpoint Longhairs can be grouped into 20 colour varieties. First there are the main colour varieties: seal, blue, chocolate, lilac, red and cream in addition to the four tortie varieties. This makes an overall number of ten varieties, each being assessed in a separate category. The other ten varieties display identical coat colours plus distinct tabby markings. They are termed Tabby or Lynx Colourpoints. They are found rather rarely, and only a few specimens are usually presented at shows. As already mentioned, they are identical to the first ten varieties except that the coat is enriched with tabby markings. The Chocolate Tabby (Lynx) Point (1) is therefore only one of the ten possible colour varieties of tabbies.

2

In Tabby Colourpoints, the shade of the body colour should be as pale as possible. The tabby pattern at the points should be distinctly visible and well broken (2), especially around the eyes, nose and on the cheeks. The same applies to the dark patches near the whiskers, namely above the eyes and on the chin. The tail should be distinctly ringed and should terminate in the appropriate colour. The front side of the legs should be marked as well, the tabby markings being most clearly seen on the forelegs. Deep blue eyes, typical of all Colourpoints, should be a matter of course.

1

Seal Point Birman

Let us begin our presentation of semi-longhairs with the Birman. At first glance it may seem that there is almost no difference between Birmans and Colourpoint Longhairs. Birmans are reminiscent of Colourpoint Longhairs primarily due to the points present on the face, legs, tail and ears and, secondly, by the coat which is quite long, especially on the ruff and tail. In fact, the coat of Birmans is not as long as that of Colourpoints and Persians. Therefore they are classified as semi-longhairs. The coat is similar in quality to that of the Turkish cat (see page 104). In addition, the Birman resembles the Turkish cat in conformation. The body should be longer than that of a Colourpoint Longhair. It should be low on its short strong legs. The tail should also be a little bit longer than in Colourpoints. Most Birmans hold their tails upright, just like squirrels do. The head shape is not like that of Persians. Although the head of a Birman is wide and round with full cheeks, the nose is longer than that of a Persian, and the nose break is indistinct or lacking. The eyes are perfectly round, though relatively small. They should be brilliant blue to sapphire.

You can see at a glance that the paws of Birmans are tipped with white. This is known as the gloves (2). On the hind paws the gloves should extend up the back of the hock to a point termed the laces. The hind paws of a Birman thus remind many of spurred boots (3, 4). This colouring and its symmetry is of great relevance when assessing cats at shows.

Colour varieties of Birmans are analogous to those of Colourpoint Longhairs or Siamese. The Seal Point (1) is the most widespread colouring. The colour at the points is as for Colourpoints or Siamese.

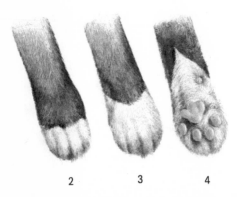

Apart from Birmans, semi-longhairs include among their number Turkish Cats, Norwegian Forest Cats, Balinese, Maine Coons and Somalis. The semi-longhair coat is distinguished from that of Persians by the absence of down hair and for this reason it seems to be less

2   3   4

1

dense. Originally, the breeds mentioned were classed among longhaired cats. As the unfair competition with Persians and Colourpoint Longhairs was a handicap to these cats, they were granted a separate class during the late 1970s. Nowadays, as well as the 'best longhair', the 'best semi-longhair' is selected at many shows.

Blue Point Birman

Birmans make very affectionate pets. When addressed by humans, they respond in a soft and quiet voice. During the period of oestrus they are more noisy, just like Siamese. Connoisseurs of the breed say that Birmans should not be bred in families with children, as they are not able to cope with children's boisterousness, which makes them become either shy or aggressive. As regards food, Birmans are rather fastidious and are not generally heavy eaters. They like to be warm, thriving best at a temperature of 22 to 24 °C (72—75 °F). As with all breeds with points the Birman's colouring is rather dependent upon temperature and air humidity. The coat and points of Birmans bred under cool and humid conditions tend to turn dark. The same thing happens to animals which are moved into different conditions of temperature and air humidity. Occasionally, their points can be almost invisible. Blue Point Birmans (1) are the most dependent upon climatic conditions. Nutrition is another vital factor determining the coat colour. Birmans should be offered mostly fresh food rich in vitamins. Dry and artificial foods are not recommended.

2

Birmans have a unique colouring among feline breeds. The body colour of a Birman, especially during the first two years of its life, should be beige with a golden hue. This makes the Birman very attractive, especially when it moves. As the fur is free from a woolly undercoat and does not have the tendency to tangle and knot, routine care is quite easy. Birmans can also be allowed out of doors without any detrimental effect upon the

quality of their coat. When compared
with Persians, there is a clear difference
in the shape of the head when viewed in
profile (2). The skull shape shows
a longish nose and a rather flat and low
forehead, which is considered a fault in
Persians.

1

Chocolate Point Birman

The Birman is also known as the Sacred Cat of Burma. Its origin is described in one of the most beautiful legends about animals, which exists in several versions. In the days before the coming of Buddha, there lived at the Temple of Lao-Tsun in the mountains of Indochina an old and wise monk called Mun Ha. He devoted his life to the sapphire-eyed Tsun-Kyan-Kse, the goddess of the migration of souls. Mun Ha had a white male cat with orange eyes, whose name was Sinh. One day, the temple was attacked by raiders. Mun Ha and the other monks found shelter in the sanctuary of Tsun-Kyan-Kse, but he died of shock there. As he was dying, his faithful companion Sinh leapt upon his white head. At this moment, monks saw a miracle — the old man's soul entered the cat. The goddess granted the cat her own godly golden colour. The paws, which rested on the old man's head, remained white at the tips. The cat's eyes became sapphire-blue like those of the goddess. They shone brightly, facing one of the gates to the temple. The other priests then quickly closed the gate. The invaders thus did not succeed in conquering the temple. All the other cats kept in the temple took on the same colouring, which was passed on to their offspring.

The historical evidence, scant as it is, at least corroborates the story of the Birman's south-east Asian origin. The first pair of Birmans were brought from there to France by Major Gordon Russell in 1919. However, their offspring did not survive. In 1925, another pair of cats was sent from Burma to France. These probably gave rise to all Birmans found today. There are other versions accounting for the Birman's origin, but it is probably true to say that they all spread from France to the other countries where they are bred at present. Their breeding increased after World War II.

During the 1960s they were brought to the United States, receiving recognition in 1967.

Seal Point and Blue Point are the original Birman colours. Chocolate Points (1) and Lilac Points (see page 94) were recognized only recently, so far remaining rather rare.

1

Lilac Point Birman

At present, four colour varieties are recognized by the standard. The Seal Point Birman must have the muzzle and paw pads toning in with the dark brown colour of the points. The Blue Point Birman should have a grey-blue muzzle and paw pads. The Chocolate Point Birman should have pads and points of warm milk chocolate colour. The Lilac Point Birman (1, 2) has lavender-pink paw pads and muzzle. Pink colour on the paw pads is acceptable in all four varieties.

Birmans are relatively uncommon because they are rather difficult to breed. Only perfect specimens of Birmans can be used for breeding, as crossings with any other breed result in a loss of a number of characteristic traits, particularly the white gloves. The gloves are determined by a recessive gene, which manifests itself only when carried by both males and females. Consequently, Birmans cannot be mated to other breeds in order to improve the other traits, which then easily become less prominent. These include the type, as well as the quality of the coat and eye colour. When a Birman is mated to another breed, the kittens are born without the gloves.

2

All Birman kittens are born uniformly pale, with the colour of the points entirely indiscernible. The first hint of colour does not begin to develop until the fourth week after birth. First it appears on the nose and ears and later on the legs and tail. Colour points are first recognized in Seal Points and Blue Points. It takes longer for the points colour to appear in Chocolate and Lilac

Point Birmans. The mask of an adult
Birman covers the face and ears without
the pencilling between, whereas in
kittens, the points on the face and ears
are separated from each other, being
banded with various colours. Along with
the fluffy hair between the ears, this
feature is typical of young animals.

1

Ragdoll

Since the time the Ragdoll appeared (during the late 1960s), there has remained a great deal of controversy among specialists over its recognition as a separate breed or variety. The Ragdoll Cat Association in California is at pains to achieve a full establishment of the breed and thus promote its official recognition. The breeding of Ragdolls is carefully controlled and recorded the world over, but the breed has not yet been recognized by most associations.

The breed is purported to derive from a white Persian female mated to a Birman male. Before the first Ragdoll was born, the mother had been severely injured in a road accident. Allegedly, the accident caused the essential change in the character of her unborn offspring.

Ragdolls mature as late as three to four years old, coming into heat only once a year, in the spring. The fact that the heat is confined to a particular season is probably a consequence of their body temperature, which is higher than in other cats. Thus, Ragdolls are more resistant to various feline infections.

Ragdoll fanciers describe the cat as the closest one can get to a human baby while still being an animal. Many cat connoisseurs, however, do not recognize Ragdolls, claiming that they have lost the feline characteristics that make a cat so attractive.

Ragdolls have quite a long body, a sturdy head, short legs and longish tail. The eyes are blue. The fur is long and thick, with the undercoat well developed. As regards the coat colour the Ragdoll represents a mix between the Birman and the Bicoloured Longhair (Parti-coloured Persian). The Ragdoll has a coloured

2

mask on the face, which, however, is not uniform; white patches or bands are acceptable. As with Birmans, there should be white gloves on the paws. The tail may be tipped with white. The all-over-white back can exhibit well-defined coloured patches, matching the colour of the mask. There are four varieties of Ragdolls — seal (1), blue (2), chocolate and lilac.

1

Somali Ruddy

Hardly any feline breed has been the subject of as much controversy as the Somali. Although already widely distributed throughout the world, many cat fanciers' associations hesitated about recognizing the Somali as a separate breed. The championship status was opposed principally by breeders of shorthaired Abyssinian cats, who claimed the Somali to be nothing but an Abyssinian with a bad coat. The longhaired mutants frequently appearing unexpectedly in Abyssinian litters and, being selected as non-standard, actually constituted the basis of the Somali breed. As recently as 1967, a New Jersey breeder called Evelyn Magus attempted selective breeding of the mutants. She gave the breed its name after the country bordering Abyssinia (now Ethiopia), in order to underline the close relationship between the two variants of a single breed — the longhaired and the short-haired. In 1972 she took the initiative in establishing the Somali Cat Club. It is greatly to the credit of this club that Somalis became distributed almost worldwide. However, it was not until 1979 that they received recognition in the United States. They were recognized by the FIFe as late as 1982.

2

Somalis are, in fact, long-coated Abyssinians. They are classed among the semi-longhairs, for their coat is not as long as that of true longhaired breeds. The heavily ticked, soft and silky coat is the most attractive trait of the Somali breed. Instead of the maximum four rings of ticking on each guard and awn hair of an Abyssinian, there are as many as 12 heavily pigmented rings (2). The eyes may either be brilliant green or deep amber.

The Somali Ruddy (1) is the most common variety. It should be a rich golden-brown ticked with black. The brick red muzzle should be rimmed with black. The paw pads may be black or brown. In comparison with the shorthaired Abyssinian, the Somali seems to be browner, due to its longer coat.

Somalis are very gentle, lively, companionable and playful cats; they even like to retrieve things. They have a soft and quiet voice. They cannot tolerate small, restricted spaces.

1

Somali Sorrel

Somalis can be divided into eight colour varieties identical to those of Abyssinians. Apart from the Somali Ruddy (see page 98), Somali Sorrels (1) are bred quite frequently, being termed alternatively Cinnamon Somalis or Russet Somalis. The coppery-red ground colour is ticked with chocolate brown. The muzzle is rich red, possibly rimmed with brown; the paw pads are pink.

Recently, six more varieties were recognized. The Somali Blue is similar in appearance to the ruddy specimens, except that the coat has a grey-blue tone with steel-blue ticking. Except for the blue-grey rim, the muzzle has the same colour as that of the Somali Ruddy. The paw pads of the Somali Sorrel are blue-grey, too. The Somali Beige Fawn is the second new variety. Here the ground colour is dull beige ticked with a deeper cream shade. The muzzle is pink with 'old-rose' rimming, the same shade being found on the paw pads. Four more varieties of Somalis Silver are known.

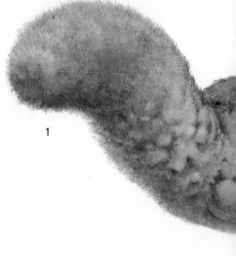

Somalis usually have small litters, bearing on average about three to four kittens, with males prevailing. Kittens are born with a grey to black shading on their bodies. Until they are one month old the fur on the forehead, neck and back remains fluffy and relatively short, as with Abyssinians; it is longer on hindlegs only. By the fifteenth week the coat gradually turns paler, showing the first ticked hair. Somali cats only achieve the fully ticked colouring at about a year, but for the most part it takes almost two years

1

for the coat to develop fully. This is even longer than with Abyssinians.

The coat of Somali cats does not need special care. It is easy to groom. The undercoat has a tendency towards becoming too dry. Somali cats should therefore be offered sufficient amounts of fat to prevent the hair from becoming brittle as well as to prevent the coat becoming dull. For the proper ticking to develop a dash of powdered sweet paprika should be added to the cat's food.

Balinese

The body type of the Balinese (1) is identical to that of Siamese cats. For many years, longhaired kittens appeared in Siamese litters. They were at first selected against and regarded as undesirable. In 1963, however, two American breeders, Helen Smith and Marion Dorsey, established a new pedigree breed, actively selecting for longhaired Siamese kittens. At the very beginning, Balinese were called 'longhaired Siamese', later being renamed to receive recognition as the Balinese. In the United States, breeders of Balinese cats associate in a special club. The club issues a specialized magazine and, to their credit, the new Balinese breed has an increasing circle of admirers. In the United States, Balinese cats have been recognized since 1970; in Europe since 1983 and in Britain since 1984.

Each new breed has a special charm and merits of its own, and Balinese cats are no exception. The Balinese shares the body type and colour pattern of the Siamese, the only difference being found in the length of the coat. The slender body is set on long legs. The tail is long and pointed. The head (2) is wedge-shaped, with large ears. The outer profile of the ears enhances the compact, wedge-shaped look of the head. The nose should be long, straight or slightly bulging, and the muzzle should be small. The brilliant blue eyes are almond-shaped, slanting towards the nose.

2

The coat of the Balinese is shorter than that of the other semi-longhairs, even on the ruff. The fur is extra soft, almost plushy, and without an undercoat. It is easy to keep groomed. The coat colour of the Balinese corresponds to that of the Siamese. Although they are only found in the four main colour varieties, a total number of 18 varieties is recognized (see the section on Siamese varieties). In the

United States, only the seal, blue, chocolate and lilac points colours are recognized as being Balinese, the other colour varieties, especially the unicoloured Orientals, being known as Javanese, after the island of Java.

1

Turkish Cat (Turkish Van)

The Turkish is not a 'man-made' breed. It is just a pedigree pet kept in the south-eastern province of Turkey, in the area of the lake Van. This is why it is sometimes called the Turkish Van. In 1955, a pair of these cats was taken from their homeland to Europe by the English breeder Laura Lushington. Later, she brought three more specimens. By 1969 Turkish cats became widespread to such a degree that they were given recognition in Britain. The FIFe recognized them in 1971.

The body is long and sturdy, and set on legs of medium length. The head should be shaped like a short spindle. The nose break, if any, should be very indistinct. The relatively large, well-feathered ears are set close together on the head. This feature reminds many of the Angora, once a widespread type of longhaired cat. Turkish cats are similar in their appearance to Angoras. The most obvious difference between the two is found in the quality of the coat. In Turkish cats, the guard and awn hairs are very soft, often reaching a length of 10—15 cm (4—6 in). As the fur is free from the woolly undercoat, the slender body is clearly visible. The coat colour should be a shining white except for the auburn-red (1) or cream (2) patches on the forehead, between the eyes and ears. The bushy tail should show distinct darker rings, auburn or rich cream in colour. The eyes may be orange or blue. The odd-eyed variety also occurs and is accepted. As with White Selfs, one eye is orange and the other is blue.

Turkish cats enjoy being in the water. They love to swim, enjoy being bathed and sometimes even catch fish. Small kittens show this enthusiasm for water, too. The kittens are born rather well-developed and with their coat already coloured. They open the eyes as early as the fourth day after birth. By the third week they are toilet trained and therefore can be kept indoors quite easily. Soon after birth, however, they should be encouraged to become used to human company. The breeder must handle them and pet them frequently, otherwise they will become wild and untamable.

2

1

Norwegian Forest Cat with Agouti Factor

The Norwegian Forest Cat is another breed with a semi-longhair coat. There are several hypotheses accounting for its origin. Most likely, Angoras were brought by ships from Italy to Norway during the 16th century. They adapted themselves to the harsh climatic conditions, which exerted an influence on the quality of their coat. They used to climb trees in order to hunt for prey. Since that time, they have retained very strong retractile claws (2). It seems likely that no more Norwegian Forest Cats exist in the wild; there are only pedigree specimens in Norway today. According to the records, Norwegian Forest Cats have been bred since 1930 and they were exhibited before World War II. After the war, Norwegian breeders produced about 200 specimens and these cats constituted the basic stock of the breed. Norwegian Forest Cats finally received recognition in 1977. Since 1981 they have been assessed in two varieties: ticked (with Agouti Factor, 1) and non-ticked (without Agouti Factor). Since 1985 specimens with (1), or without white spotting, are distinguished within each variety.

Another theory claims the Norwegian Forest Cat to be a mutation of the European Wild Cat (*Felis silvestris grampia*). Today this subspecies can be found living in the wild in Scotland. Vikings could have brought it from there to Norway. The hypothesis is corroborated by old engravings, which depict the goddess Freya in a carriage drawn by cats similar in appearance to Norwegian Forest Cats.

retracted claw

protracted claw

In order to preserve the purity of the pedigree breed, an exception was made as regards the move by Norwegian breeders not to permit novice classes for Norwegian Forest Cats at shows. New specimens are accepted only after having been thoroughly assessed and accepted by the board of Norwegian breeders. The board only approves specimens similar in their appearance to Norwegian Forest Cats. In this way, they ensure the purity of the breed.

2

1

Norwegian Forest Cats are
affectionate and rather playful,
frequently remaining so well into old age.
At the same time, they may exhibit
a strong streak of individualism, even by
feline standards.

Norwegian Forest Cat without Agouti Factor

Norwegian Forest Cats are sturdily built. As already mentioned, the rather long body is set on legs of medium length. The back legs are slightly longer than the front legs. The relatively small head is triangular in shape, with a powerful chin, and the rather long nose is straight without any nose break. This is known as the Roman nose (2). The ears are long and set high on the head, the outer margins being in line with the cheeks. The ear tufts should be well developed on the ear tips, as with the lynx. (Ear tufts are found in all members of the cat family. They are either short, or are removed by selecting against them during breeding, as with the Persians.) The tail (3) of the Norwegian Forest Cat is long and bushy and they have a special double coat. It is composed of two completely different types of fur: the long and soft undercoat is covered with the coarse and glossy outer coat which is oily and therefore water-resistant. The hair is long, reaching almost to the ground on both sides, thus resembling a mantle. This coat type is only found in Norwegian Forest Cats. The breed is further distinguished by having rather long and thick hairs arranged in triangles on both cheeks as well as by rich fur on the haunches, where it forms a pair of 'breeches'. There is no restriction on the eye or coat colours acceptable in Norwegian Forest Cats. The only requirement for the eye colour is that it should tone with the ground colour of the coat. Two variants of the Norwegian Forest Cat without Agouti Factor, in other words without ticking (1), occur: with or without white spotting.

2

1

In Norwegian Forest Cats, the quality and length of the coat varies. There is often a large difference between the winter fur and the summer coat. During the summer, they usually have a short coat, almost without a ruff. There is no thick undercoat in summer; it only begins to grow during the autumn period of moulting. Kittens only develop the coarse outer coat at the age of three to five months.

The coat of Norwegian Forest Cats requires a different method of preparation for the show than that of other breeds. Before the show, cats should be bathed once or twice — preferably several days in advance, to enable the outer coat to become well-oiled again. The powder should be applied just before the show, when making the final arrangements to the ruff and underside of the tail.

3

Maine Coon

The Maine Coon (1) is native to North America. The English name of the breed emphasizes the cat's similarity to the racoon, especially in the bushy tail. It is a large and sturdy cat. Males weigh up to 7 kg (15 lb), and sometimes more. Females weigh as much as 5 kg (11 lb). A considerable resemblance between the Maine Coon and the Norwegian Forest Cat indicates a common ancestry. The Maine Coon most likely originates from longhaired mutants of European cats which were brought from Europe by the early American settlers. Under harsh climatic conditions in Canada they developed into a separate breed. According to another theory, the Maine Coon is a descendant of the cats belonging to Marie Antoinette, Queen of France. When planning her escape to Canada, the Queen allegedly sent her furniture and cats there in advance, Norwegian Forest Cats and their progeny included. These gave rise to the Maine Coon breed.

On the American continent, Maine Coons were valued as catchers of vermin more than 200 years ago. There is reliable evidence that agricultural shows featured Maine Coons as early as 1860, at the time when there were no special cat shows. At the turn of the century, however, interest in the breed waned for about 50 years until the establishment of the American Central Maine Cat Club. To its credit, pedigree records were re-established and the breed was given recognition in 1967. Maine Coons have been bred the world over ever since.

The fur of Maine Coons is thick, glossy and rather coarse, frequently free from an undercoat, and increasing in length towards the tail. Consequently, there is almost no ruff, the fur being particularly long on the sides and stomach as well as on the haunches, where it forms a pair of 'breeches'. Any coat colour is permitted except the point colours, where it must conform to that found in Colourpoint Longhairs (Himalayans) or Birmans. The head of the Maine Coon is relatively small. The square cheeks are set high, with a distinct muzzle pinch. The large ears are set wide apart. The eyes are slightly slanting. There is no restriction on the eye colour, but green is preferred to other colours at shows. Whatever the colour, it should match the overall tone of the fur. The legs are long with strong paws. The hair tufts between the toes should be well developed.

Maine Coons are endearing and playful cats, enjoying human company. They develop slowly and may not achieve their full size until they are four years old.

Black British Shorthair

The Black British Shorthair is among the most common colour varieties. Its coat should be black to the roots with no sign of rustiness or greyish tinge. Any white hair as well as hints of tabby markings are considered a definite fault. When exposed to the sun, the fur of a top black cat can frequently develop a brownish hue. As cats are known to enjoy sunbathing, it is recommended to keep a show cat away from the sun before the show. The muzzle and paw pads of Black British Shorthairs are black, too. The desirable eye colour is deep orange to copper, although the eyes of black cats are frequently greenish (2), yellowish (3) or orange with traces of green. It is usually impossible for cats with such eyes to win a show prize.

In the Middle Ages, shorthaired black cats were thought to bring bad luck. They were regarded as companions of devils and witches. This is why they used to be burnt or otherwise exterminated. In some parts of the world, for example in the United States, the negative attitude towards black cats has survived up to the present time. On the other hand, in Britain black cats are considered to bring luck.

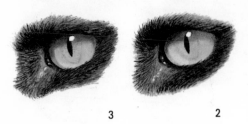

3   2

Kittens of Black British Shorthairs frequently show imperfections in coat colouring, such as brownish, rusty or grey patches as well as faint tabby markings. They do not disappear until six or seven months of age. The coat turns black at maturity. Sometimes, its colour is even better than that of the kitten, which was deep black from the very beginning. As with longhaired cats, by incorporating the dilute gene it is possible to breed blue, chocolate and lilac varieties. The last two varieties so far remain rather rare.

1

White British Shorthair

You can see at a glance that White British Shorthairs (1, 2) are most attractive cats, especially when their coat is white without the slightest suggestion of yellow. Strangely enough, the pure white specimens are not to be found frequently, although they are quite common with other breeds. This phenomenon so far remains unexplained.

As already mentioned with Persians, there are three colour varieties of White British Shorthairs recognized by show standards. They are distinguished by the eye colour: Copper-eyed or Orange-eyed White Shorthair, Blue-eyed White Shorthair, Odd-eyed White Shorthair (one eye orange, the other blue).

British Shorthairs of all colour varieties are medium to large cats. Their muscular body is heavily or massively built. The full chest is set on short legs with the feet strong and well rounded. The tail is short and thick, with a rounded tip. The head is paid particularly thorough attention at shows. It should be round, massive and well set on the short and strong neck. The chin should be perfectly developed. The nose is short, wide and straight, without any nose break. The ears of the British Shorthair are short and wide, and slightly rounded at the tips. It is not only the colour and pattern of the coat, but also the quality of its soft and plushy texture which is subject to assessment at shows. It should be short and thick, but not too close-lying. The undercoat is well developed, being of the same length as the outer coat. Where the outer coat is longer than the undercoat, the fur is too close-lying, which is regarded as a fault. The hair should be well coloured to the roots, except for the tipped varieties.

3

Judging at shows involves assessing an animal's overall condition, including its suppleness and litheness. An animal's overall appearance, the proportions between the respective parts of the body as well as the quality of a breeder's care are taken into consideration.

The kittens of White British Shorthairs are white, showing a blackish or grey smudge (3) on the forehead between the ears until one year of age.

1

2

Blue British Shorthair (British Blue)

British Shorthairs occur in a great number of colour varieties. The British Blue (1) is a typical representative of the breed. It has been known for many years, being first exhibited in London as early as 1880. The early pedigree records date back to the year 1898. In the British Isles, the British Blue is the most popular variety among British Shorthairs. All shades of grey-blue or grey colour are permitted, but the light grey-blue pastel shade is favoured nowadays, as the pastel colour makes most dramatic contrast with the brilliant copper or orange eyes. In cat terminology, however, they are termed blue. (A similar colour harmony is found in the Cream British Shorthair, 2.)

The British Blue is very similar to the Chartreux (see page 146). Until quite recently, the Chartreux was identified with the British Blue, being regarded as a single breed by the FIFe. Since the breeds were officially separated in 1967, the standard specifies that the British Blue is less stocky, having broader cheeks, smaller ears and slightly longer legs than the Chartreux. The main difference is in the coat. It is rather short, soft and close-lying in contrast to the Chartreux, the coat of which is thick and stands out from the body. However, most blue shorthaired cats found on the Continent nowadays represent a type intermediate between the two breeds.

2

Breeders do not always succeed at breeding a British Shorthair showing a perfect coat colour, be it the British Blue or any other colour variety. Animals usually show at least faint hints of tabby markings on the legs. Kittens sometimes develop the markings or even a regular tabby pattern on the back. As the pattern

116

tends to disappear at maturity, it is not necessary to select against such specimens. In particular cases, however, the pattern can reappear temporarily under special circumstances, such as during extremely hot or cold weather.

1

Blue Cream British Shorthair

The Blue Cream British Shorthair (1) is one of the rarest varieties and this makes its striking appearance even more unusual. Requirements for distribution of the colours in the coat are as for the blue cream varieties of other breeds. In Britain and on the Continent, the light blue and cream hairs should be softly intermingled, thus creating an impression 'as if the cat was painted in water-colours'. The same applies to the tail (2), which is quite frequently not well intermingled. The animal has an overall bluish hue, as there should theoretically be two blue hairs for each cream hair. Cats with a cream blaze or streak on the forehead are said to be favoured by judges at some shows, although according to the British Standard the colours should be softly mingled, not patched. In America, by contrast, Blue Cream Shorthairs are required to have clear blue and cream patches all over the coat and the blaze is desirable. The muzzle and paw pads should be pink, blue-grey or pink spotted with blue-grey. The eyes should be copper or deep orange, as with most British Shorthairs.

2

As the coat of Blue Creams should be softly intermingled, any suggestion of tabby markings or pattern is regarded as a great fault. Consequently, mating Blue Cream females to tabby males is not recommended, for the coat colour of the offspring will undoubtedly suffer.

The Blue Cream kittens are born almost self blue, with just faint hints of the future cream hair found on very few parts of the body. The cream hair only begins to show through later. The full colour of the coat is thus reached only at about nine to ten months of age, or even later.

1

Tortoiseshell British Shorthair

In British Shorthairs, the occurrence of the tortoiseshell colouring is determined by the presence of the black and orange (red) genes (the red gene is carried on sex chromosomes). The Tortoiseshell British Shorthair should exhibit clear and defined patches of both colours, black and red (1). The most important point is the balanced ratio of colours, regardless of the size of the patches.

An elongated red marking set against the black background can sometimes be found in the centre of the forehead (2). In cat terminology, this is known as the blaze. Tortoiseshells with a blaze are particularly favoured at shows. The eye colour should be copper or deep orange, as with the other British Shorthairs. The muzzle and paw pads are black, pink or black spotted with pink.

Tortoiseshells as well as blue cream cats are female-only varieties. The gene for red colour is located on the sex chromosome X. Consequently, no males of these colour varieties are normally found and, if they are, it is a pathological case and the male is invariably sterile. In spite of this fact, there is a record of two tortoiseshell males which lived at the beginning of the century. Allegedly, they sired many litters, but it is open to some controversy whether or not they actually were real tortoiseshells.

The standard allows for a variable intensity of red shades in Tortoiseshell British Shorthairs. It is an interesting point, as in the main, the present standard corresponds to the former definition (before the year 1982). The former standard required three colours — black, red and cream.

According to the present definition, ground colours should be clear, and there should be no signs of tabby markings.

2

120

This is why tortoiseshell females should not be mated to tabby or tipped males. The possible offspring, tortoiseshell or blue cream females, could inherit the distinct tabby pattern of their father.

1

Tortoiseshell-and-white British Shorthair (Calico Shorthair)

The Tortoiseshell-and-white British Shorthair (1, 2) is a rather common variety of British Shorthair. As with other breeds, its colouring is an arrangement of black, red and white patches. Not more than two-thirds and not less than half of the cat's coat should be coloured; the rest should be white. The colours should be distributed in large and defined patches, well-separated from the white. All three colours should be found in balanced amounts on the face, back, legs and tail. Red patches should not show any tabby markings. As the red frequently occurs in two or more colour shades, former standards required black, red, cream and white colouring for the Tortoiseshell-and-white British Shorthair.

Tortoiseshell-and-white British Shorthairs are always females. No males occur, as the orange (red) gene is sex-linked. This means it is carried on the X chromosome. (Females have two and males only one X chromosome.) Females of this variety can only be mated to self males. In planned breeding, no marked or tipped males should be used for mating.

The Tortoiseshell-and-white British Shorthair was originally known as the Spanish Cat, as a naturalist of the time, Georges Buffon, believed the cat owed its colouring to the warm Spanish climate.

2

1

By special methods of mating, the black colour can be diluted to blue and red to cream, with the white remaining. Thus, a variety known as the Blue Tortoiseshell-and-white (Dilute Calico) is also obtained. Where the black is substituted by a chocolate or lilac colour and the red by cream, standards recognize the Chocolate Tortoiseshell-and-white

British Shorthair (Calico Shorthair) and the Lilac Tortoiseshell-and-white British Shorthair (Calico Shorthair).

The colours of the muzzle and paw pads of all Tortoiseshell-and-white varieties are as for tortoiseshells — pink, black or black spotted with pink.

123

Bicoloured British Shorthair

Bicoloured British Shorthairs received official recognition only recently. They were distinguished from European Shorthairs and given a standardized definition as late as 1969. Not until 1980 were they officially distinguished from the only breed recognized in the United States — the American Shorthair.

We recognize six colour varieties. The white colour occurs in combination with black (1, 2), blue, chocolate, lilac, red (3) or cream. These colour combinations are found among common rural or stray cats, which are more European than British in type. But although many bicolours exist, not every cat would conform with the requirements laid down for the animal acceptable for breeding. To correspond to the standard, the colours should be well-balanced, and the patches of colour should be clearly defined. The colour should be rich and solid, and no shading or variable colour intensity is permitted. The colours should be evenly distributed. The face, back, legs and tail should be coloured, the colour covering not more than two-thirds and not less than half of the cat's coat. The colours should be symmetrically distributed all over the face. Animals usually show a white blaze running down the centre of the forehead (3) so that the coloured part forms a kind of 'curtain'. The muzzle and paw pads are either pink or match the overall tone of the coat. Pigmented patches on the muzzle, as well as black whiskers, are considered a fault in red and cream bicolours.

3

In accordance with genetic laws, a bicoloured cat can only occur where at least one parent is a bicolour, or a Tortie-and-white (Calico). Heterozygous specimens, however, do not necessarily pass the gene for white (piebald) spotting on to the offspring. Thus, the litter of a bicolour can contain self kittens of both sexes as well as tortoiseshell females. It follows that the breeding of bicolours often takes the breeder by surprise, as he can never guess the colour of kittens in the litter. Appropriate combinations can yield as many as 16 colour varieties.

2

1

Brown Tabby British Shorthair (Mackerel)

Ancient paintings, reliefs and mosaics show that tabby markings were almost invariably present in the coat of early domestic cats of all colours. It is the trait inherited from the cat's ancestors, the subspecies of the European Wild Cat (*Felis silvestris silvestris*) as well as the African Wild Cat (*Felis silvestris lybica*). They are believed to have given rise to all present-day shorthaired breeds and colour varieties which developed over the course of centuries.

Until the 16th century, only shorthaired cats — mostly with tabby markings — seem to have been known in Europe. Tabby patterns are of several types. The mackerel (or tiger) striped tabby is the original and basic tabby pattern. The blotched ('classic') or standard tabby pattern is a mutation, which evolved later. The pattern was not known until the 17th century. It probably appeared first in Europe, since cats with a blotched tabby pattern are not yet well established in the Far East and India. A selection for blotched tabbies has led to the development of the spotted cat. This type of pattern is rare, probably because the pattern did not develop spontaneously, being instead a result of deliberate breeding.

Shorthaired cats occur in a wide range of breeds nowadays. There is a number of colour modifications, which were recently specified on the basis of modern research in genetics. The same applies to the British breed. All colour varieties, self cats included, were derived and bred from tabbies.

The ground colour of the Brown Tabby British Shorthair (1, mackerel) should be a warm golden brown with a distinct tabby pattern. The brick red muzzle should be rimmed with black, and the paw pads should be black or dark brown. The eyes should be copper or deep orange. The eyelids are rimmed with black.

Mackerel tabbies are among the most common cats. Brown Tabby to Brown Tabby and Red Tabby to Red Tabby matings continued through generations led to indistinct or even blurred tabby markings. In England, for example, most rural domestic cats (2) are of this pattern type. A cat called Mickey, the registered

126

2

'employee' of Shepard and Sons warehouse in Burscough, Lancashire, is said to have been of the same colouring. He is claimed to have killed 22,000 mice during his life.

1

Brown Tabby British Shorthair (Blotched or 'Classic')

At present, there are seven colour varieties of Tabby British Short-hairs recognized by the standard. The type of the pattern laid upon the ground colour is prescribed by the standard, being classified as the mackerel, blotched or spotted tabby pattern. In cases where the tabby pattern does not correspond to the standard requirements, the cat cannot be considered seriously for showing in breed classes. Although there are many tabbies about, their colouring is mostly non-standard. As a consequence of free and uncontrolled mating, certain colour characteristics which are determined by dominant genes usually become manifest. From the point of view of breeding, however, these traits are undesirable. For example, the coat of a tabby may show white areas of variable size.

White patches or separate white hairs are definitely undesirable with all breeds of British Shorthairs. The 'wrongly' coloured hair is most frequently found on the chin, chest and legs, and cause the dis-qualification of an otherwise excellent animal. The white patches are determined by the presence of a dominant gene which usually mani-fests itself in the coat of the offspring. Prescribed amounts of white hair are only desirable in the White Shorthair, all bicoloured varieties as well as in the tortie-and-white and blue cream-and-white varieties.

The blotched tabby pattern (a Blotched Brown Tabby British Shorthair, 1, 2) is more common now in Europe than the mackerel type. In Australia, blotched specimens are also more common.

2

Kittens of all the tabby varieties are born rather dark, with their coats showing concentrated tabby patterns. The pattern becomes less dense as the kittens grow up. This fact should be taken into account when selecting the kittens for further breeding.

1

Silver Tabby British Shorthair (Mackerel)

The uniform pattern on the head (2) and chest is a basic trait found in all tabby varieties, be it the mackerel, blotched or spotted type. In the centre of the forehead there are several transverse stripes, the longest running up to the top of the head. The shorter stripes are arranged into a pattern resembling the letter M. A clearly defined pair of spectacles is usually seen around the eyes. Running at an angle beneath eyes, the cheeks are crossed by two or three spirals or swirls. The chest is decorated with two unbroken lines known as the 'mayoral chains'. The front of the forelegs is regularly ringed.

All the traits mentioned are common to all pattern types of tabbies. The difference between the patterns is found on the back and sides. The Mackerel Tabby should have three longitudinal stripes on the back, the middle one running down to the tail. Vertical stripes run down from the lines on the back. They should be more or less horizontal and distinctly separated from each other. The tail should be similarly ringed and tipped with the appropriate dark colour. The blotched tabby pattern begins right behind the head. The markings on the shoulders and front haunches as well as on the back and sides should be arranged into a compact whorled pattern roughly resembling butterfly wings in shape. Finally, the spotted type is similar to the Mackerel Tabby, but the vertical stripes should be broken into separate spots. The spots should be well defined, by no means running together.

2

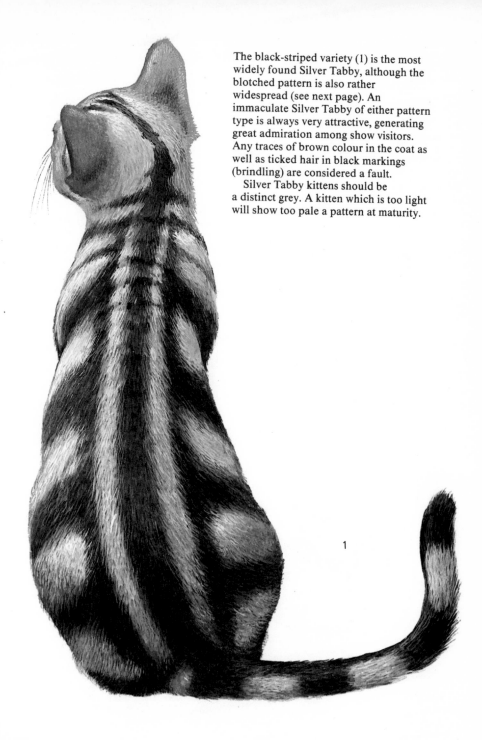

The black-striped variety (1) is the most widely found Silver Tabby, although the blotched pattern is also rather widespread (see next page). An immaculate Silver Tabby of either pattern type is always very attractive, generating great admiration among show visitors. Any traces of brown colour in the coat as well as ticked hair in black markings (brindling) are considered a fault.

Silver Tabby kittens should be a distinct grey. A kitten which is too light will show too pale a pattern at maturity.

1

Silver Tabby British Shorthair (Standard or 'Classic')

The Silver Tabby pattern differs widely from other tabby varieties of the British Shorthairs. There are four colour shades: Black Silver Tabby with black markings (the classic type, 1); Blue Silver Tabby with blue markings; Chocolate (Chestnut) Silver Tabby (2) with brown markings; and Lilac (Lavender) Silver Tabby with lilac markings. The eye colour of all Silver Tabbies is different from that of other tabbies. It is green or yellow, while the eyes of the other varieties should be copper or deep orange.

The four analogous tabby varieties should be distinguished from Silver Tabbies. These are the Brown Tabby British Shorthair (see pages 126 and 128), Blue Tabby British Shorthair (see page 132), Chocolate (Chestnut) Tabby British Shorthair showing dark brown markings laid upon the brown ground coat and, finally, the Lilac Tabby British Shorthair, exhibiting the lilac coat with contrast ice grey markings of pinkish hue.

No variety of European Shorthairs exhibiting chocolate or lilac shade is recognized by the standard, although such animals are to be found. The European Shorthair, as already mentioned, is found in colour varieties corresponding to those of the British Shorthair.

2

The coat of British Shorthairs requires no special care. Weekly combing and grooming is normally sufficient, especially when there is no moulting. As British Shorthairs are mostly allowed to go outdoors, a bath is sometimes needed in case they are very dirty. Just before the judging at a show, the coat can be made to look glossy by smoothing it with a bare hand or a leather glove.

1

Blue Tabby British Shorthair

The 'classic' Blue Tabby (1, 2) is another colour variety of the British Shorthairs. The blue variety was recognized only recently. Strangely enough, the early recognized specimens did not show the mackerel pattern, only the 'classic' one. The ground colour of the coat is ivory with a touch of blue and the markings are dark blue. The shell muzzle is rimmed with dark blue. The same applies to the eyelids. The paw pads are blue-grey. However, the colouring corresponding to the standard requirements is found only rarely. In rural areas, one may come across many specimens showing a colouring similar to the Blue Tabby British Shorthair. However, there are usually visible traces of other colours in their coat, particularly white (3). Alternatively, the dark blue markings may not be coloured thoroughly to the hair roots, thus creating a slight tint all over the surface of the coat. Such animals are no longer suitable for breeding, although they may have a perfect head shape or body conformation.

3

Although there are no problems as regards the breeding of British Shorthairs, breeders try to find new ways of improving their colours. Occasionally, British Shorthairs used to be mated to Persians in order to achieve perfect colours. Apart from the actual improvement of coat colour, the method brought about many negative effects such as the atypical coat structure, a tendency to show a nose break, running eyes or even a change in the cat's character. The lively but even-tempered British Shorthair is changed into a lethargic and easily frightened cat. Therefore, these experiments can by no means be recommended.

The American (Domestic) Shorthair (see page 148) was probably bred by similar methods. It is rather difficult to distinguish the breed from the British Shorthair and to tell the difference from the European Shorthair is even more complicated, as ancestors of the American Shorthair were brought to America by the early colonists.

2

1

A particularly close resemblance to the
American Shorthair is visible in those
specimens of British and European
Shorthairs which have ancestors of other
breeds recorded.

Red Tabby British Shorthair

For each colour variety, the ground colour of the coat as well as the colour of the pattern are strictly specified by the standard. All seven tabby varieties have the ticking well developed in the ground colour of their coat. Red and Cream Tabbies are the only unticked varieties. The ground colour should be red or cream with deep red or deep cream tabby markings.

The standard further specifies the eye colour, the colour of the eyelids, muzzle and paw pads, which should always tone in with the ground colour of the coat. When a specimen does not conform to the requirement, the imperfect colour combination is penalized by judges. The muzzle of the Red Tabby British Shorthair is brick red. The rim of the muzzle should match the colour of the markings on the back. The muzzle of the 'classic' Cream Tabby British Shorthair (2) can show different shades of pink, the rim matching the colour of the markings. Some varieties constitute an exception. For example, the markings of the Lilac Tabby British Shorthair are grey with a lilac shade, while the eyelids are rimmed with lavender pink.

2

The mackerel Red Tabby British Shorthair (1) is common throughout Europe. It is interesting to note that there are mostly male specimens in this variety, although Red Tabby females occur as well. In Britain, this variety has often been described as a ginger or marmalade cat.

1

Spotted British Shorthair

Spotted British Shorthairs so far remain rarities. There is evidence that they were common at one time, but they disappeared suddenly and did not reappear until the 1960s. Their reappearance brought about a quick official recognition in 1966.

The back and sides of the spotted cat should be covered with a large number of spots, which should not necessarily be round. They may be oblong or rosette-shaped, but they should have a uniform shape in the same cat. Some spots may merge into stripes or become indistinctly separated, giving an impression of a broken mackerel pattern, but this is considered a definite fault. The importance which used to be attached to the quality of the pattern is best illustrated by the number of points allocated by the standard. Formerly, the quality of the pattern could be allocated as much as half the total number of points, while the present standard does not regard the spotted cat as an exception, judging it according to the same scale as the other British Shorthairs.

As regards the colouring, all colour shades are permitted for the ground colour as well as for the markings. As in both the mackerel and blotched type cats, ticking is well developed in the ground colour of the coat except in Red and Cream Tabbies. This is clearly visible on the picture of the Black-spotted Silver Tabby British Shorthair (1) as well as on the Blue-spotted Silver Tabby British Shorthair (2).

2

If you are looking for an attractive and affectionate companion, it is probably the British Shorthair that will best suit you of all feline breeds. At first sight you would certainly not expect such a combination of lively temperament and endearing character in its robust body. The British Shorthair is calm but not indifferent, and neither shy nor blindly trusting. It is affectionate but not obtrusive. It senses when it is welcome and when it is not. To show its charm and undemanding character it requires only a peaceful and caring environment.

1

British Tipped Shorthair (Chinchilla)

British Shorthairs can be found almost everywhere, exhibiting a diversity of colour varieties. They are actually the most common cats, being particularly appreciated at places where humans need assistance in catching vermin. In comparison with other breeds these cats look the most 'ordinary', although many of them could have been purebred specimens with the appropriate pedigree and with many champions among their ancestors. The only prerequisite is to conform with the standard laid down for any of the 76 varieties of British Shorthairs or the other 41 varieties of the related European Shorthairs.

Only a few British Shorthairs have more than four generations of ancestors recorded. The reason for this is a lack of interest on the part of the public. Little interest is shown in British Shorthairs by breeders, in spite of their undisputed charm. An enthusiastic breeder faces another problem. During the centuries of free and uncontrolled reproduction, the traits which are passed on to the offspring have become genetically encoded even in well-selected, immaculate specimens. According to current standards, these traits are regarded as faulty and atypical. This applies especially to traces of white hair on the chin, chest and tail tip, which are rather difficult to suppress.

2

An attentive reader has probably already recognized that the British Shorthair is available in a larger number of standardized varieties than the European Shorthair, although the breeds closely resemble each other. In the British breed, the number of varieties is increased by the British Tipped Shorthair (1) and the derived British Shaded Silver Shorthair (the blue variant, 2). Their colourings are true copies of the Chinchilla (Silver

140

1

Persian) and the Silver Shaded Persian, but in the shorthaired form. Their coat is white. The fur on the head, ears, back, sides and tail is interwoven with black, blue, chocolate or lilac-tipped hair. The eye colour is an emerald green. The colour of the eyelids and the rim of the muzzle should match the overall tone of the variety. These animals so far remain rare.

Smoke British Shorthair

All varieties of Smoke British Shorthairs (1) are described as 'cats of contrasts'. As with the Persians of the same type, Smoke British Shorthairs should display a silvery white undercoat which should be covered with black-, blue-, chocolate- or lilac-tipped hair. There are four varieties of smokes. There are relatively large amounts of tipped hair in the coat of a smoke. It is coloured in the appropriate colour, being silvery white at the roots, just like the undercoat. When the animal is not moving it cannot be properly classified as a smoke, as the silvery undercoat can be clearly seen only when the cat is in motion. The muzzle and paw pads should tone in with the colour of the tipping. The ear tufts should be a silvery white, too. As with the other British Shorthairs, the eyes should be copper or deep orange.

Poorly developed tipping or hints of tabby markings, especially on the legs (2), are considered a definite fault with adult animals. In addition to larger amounts of grey hair, young animals show these imperfections quite often. These faults are acceptable in kittens, however, as they tend to disappear with age.

2

1

Smoke Shorthairs received preliminary recognition in the early 1970s as an experimental breed. This means that they were not eligible for an award at a show. They were given official recognition as late as 1983. Up to now, however, Smoke British Shorthairs remain rather rare. They are much more widespread among non-pedigree household pets, which by no means conform with the standard requirements.

European Shorthair

All cats which are common on the European continent can, in fact, be classed among European Shorthairs. The pictures show their cream (1) and blue (2) representatives. Nevertheless, the blue variety of the European Shorthair used to be described as the British Blue in the British Isles. The standard was not altered until 1982. In fact, the difference between the European and British Shorthair can only be told after typical representatives of both breeds have been thoroughly examined by a skilled specialist. Over the years of mutual mating, the characteristic traits of each breed became mixed together. Therefore it is actually rare to come across a perfect specimen of either breed. Most shorthairs represent a type intermediate between the European and British breed.

The body of the European cat is of medium length. The same applies to the neck, nose, ears, legs, and tail. In British cats these body features are all shorter. The largest difference is found on the head. It should be round in both breeds, showing a slightly more visible elongation in the European Shorthair. A minor difference can be found in the nose build. The standard specifies a straight nose for both breeds. However, European Shorthairs show a very shallow indentation in the area intermediate between the nose and forehead. In British Shorthairs, on the other hand, the nose break is either not present or is always considered more or less acceptable. As already mentioned, this is because an immaculate specimen of the British Shorthair is rather rare nowadays.

2

1

European Shorthairs occur in practically all the colour varieties found in other breeds. Over the years, a number of non-standardized colour combinations have appeared as the result of uncontrolled mating. Such specimens are described as household pets, being judged in a separate class at shows.

Furthermore, chocolate and lilac colours and their combinations are not recognized by the standard laid down for European Shorthairs, although the colours are standardized for other breeds. There are 41 colour varieties of European Shorthairs recognized by the current standard.

Chartreux

Chartreux cats (1) are among the oldest breeds in Europe. They were supposedly brought from Africa by Carthusian monks as long ago as 1550. They were bred in French monasteries and have remained popular in France ever since. The breed has spread worldwide, reaching the American continent in the early 1970s.

There is a number of traits which distinguish the Chartreux from the British Shorthair. Chartreux cats have a special type of coat. It is very soft, dense and glossy. The coat should not be close-set. It should stand out from the body, just like an otter's fur. This is the result of the richly developed undercoat. Any shade of blue or grey is acceptable, a light grey-blue being preferred to other colours. Adult animals should not show any tabby markings, shading or white hair.

The Chartreux is a cat of powerful, robust and muscular build. The head is round , and the chin and cheeks are well developed. The ears are characteristically pointed. They are of medium length, and covered with a fine fur. They are set high on the head, though not exactly on the top, and point forward slightly. Thus the Chartreux seems to be listening attentively. The copper or deep orange eyes are large and round.

2

1

Chartreux cats are courageous and brave, and have a reputation for being vigorous catchers of rats. They are also lively and cheerful, and always active. Cats which are allowed to go outdoors do not avoid fights with dogs. They do not particularly care about being fondled on their owner's lap, nor do they spend much time sleeping in one place, either. They purr in a loud voice, and sometimes mew in a faint voice, rather like kittens. This mewing sound seems strangely at odds with their sturdy look. Their breeders stress their intelligence.

The kittens of the Chartreux (2) are almost always born with tabby markings and a ringed tail. The markings and rings do not disappear until they are one year old. The eyes achieve the proper colour quite late, too.

American Shorthair (Domestic Shorthair)
American Wirehair

Among the shorthaired cats found in America, there are two local breeds only occurring on the American continent. These are the American (Domestic) Shorthair (2) and the American Wirehair (1). Most American cats are similar in appearance to European breeds. The question is whether or not they are identical, as only a specialist is able to distinguish the breeds. The only traits distinguishing the American Shorthair from the British breed are a relatively longer body and the slightly longer tail; the eyes slant more towards the outer edges and the ear tips are slightly rounded (their height should correspond to the width at the base). As the available specimens represent an intermediate type of cat and no perfect or 'pure' animals are found either in Europe or in America, it is practically impossible to make a clear distinction.

As with British and European Shorthairs, only specimens with appropriate coat colour corresponding to the standard are selected for further breeding. Animals of other colours can only be kept as household pets. The Red Tabby variety, which is often described as a ginger cat, sometimes acquires a brownish or cinnamon shade. The American Shorthair was recognized as a separate breed in 1965, while the British Shorthair, which is also recognized in the United States, was distinguished from the American breed as late as 1980.

The American Wirehair (1) is a mutant of the American Shorthair. It differs from the original breed by the medium-length coat of stiff hair, which is wiry on the head (the whiskers included), back, haunches and upperside of the tail. A similar coat can be found in some breeds of dogs. The hair is elastic and slightly crimped (3), sometimes forming a kind of spiral. This particular quality of the coat is outlined by the standard. The American Wirehair was given championship status by some of the American cat fanciers' associations as early as 1977.

2

3

1

Exotic Shorthair

The Exotic Shorthair (1) is among the breeds which were recognized in Britain by the CA in 1983 and by the FIFe in 1984. Although first attempts at breeding began in the United States in the 1920s, the Exotic Shorthair became a separate breed only in the mid-1960s, receiving official recognition in 1967. Many discussions preceded their recognition, as Exotic Shorthairs are the result of crossbreeding the Longhair (Persian) breed to the American Shorthair. They are, in point of fact, hybrids. Since 1977 only demonstrable hybrids have been recorded in the stock-book in the United States. From the genetic point of view, the external characteristics of the breed have not yet become fully established. In the United States, like-to-like mating is permitted only exceptionally, as the combination usually produces kittens similar in appearance to the American Shorthair. However, the main reason is that the mating results in a loss of the major trait — the intermediate-length coat (1—4 cm/½—1½ inches). The shorter coat does not turn woolly. As regards the colouring, the Exotic Shorthair is recognized in the same varieties as the Persian breed.

Exotic Shorthairs have an increasing circle of admirers. Thanks to their good-natured, playful and rather intelligent character the breed has gradually spread the world over. One could say that this is the breed of the future.

2

Exotic Shorthairs are in fact identical in terms of their body build to Persians except that they do not exhibit a long coat, one of the traits typical of Persians. Their coat is short, being slightly longer than that of shorthaired cats. On the other hand, Exotic Shorthairs have shorter coats than semi-longhairs. Their coat is soft, dense and plush — almost elastic. At first glance, one notices the head (2) and the face, showing an almost childlike expression. The head is perfectly round. The ears are pointed

1

slightly forward and are rounded. They should not protrude from the contours of the head. The eyes are wide, and set quite wide apart. The nose is short, but in contrast with Persians, the peke-faced type is not recognized. The medium-length robust body is set low on the legs. The tail is short and thick, its length being proportionate to the body size.

Scottish Fold

Many years ago, an interesting type of cat was reported to occur in China. According to cat literature, it was white, longhaired, with ears drooping forward. The mutants were claimed to occur exclusively in China. Accordingly, they used to be commonly described as Chinese cats. As recently as 1961, however, specimens showing the same departure reappeared first in Scotland and later in other countries. They gave rise to the new shorthaired breed known as the Scottish Fold (1). In spite of being relatively widespread, they have been recognized neither by the FIFe nor by the GCCF but are accepted by several American associations and in Britain by the CA.

Folded ear flaps are determined by the presence of a dominant gene. They are common in other domestic animals such as dogs, sheep, pigs etc, yet until quite recently they have not been observed in cats. Breeders distinguish between simple-folded and double-folded ears. The simple-folded ear droops forward, while the double-folded ear droops both forward and downward with the ear tip almost touching the fur on the head. If one ear remains unfolded, a cat is disqualified in a show. The ears are folded only partly at birth, the effect increasing into adulthood.

The folded ears with rounded tips should be set wide apart on the perfectly round head (2), being the most striking as well as the most attractive trait of the breed.

2

The roundness of the head is highlighted
with the wide short nose and large round
eyes, giving a somewhat smiling
expression. The short, almost cobby body
of the Scottish Fold is set on
medium-length, sturdy legs. The longish
tail is rather thick. A rounded tip to the
tail is acceptable. The ratio of length to
body size is important. The tip of the
hanging tail should precisely touch the
ground on which the cat is standing. As
with British Shorthairs, any eye and coat
colour is acceptable (except for
chocolate, lilac and points colours)
provided they match.

1

153

Manx

The tailless Manx (1) has been known for centuries. There is historical evidence that King Edward VII of England owned several Manx cats as pets. They are the result of a natural mutation, or better to say, degeneration, which occurred due to inbreeding of British Shorthairs on the Isle of Man in the Irish Sea. The feline population was cut off for a long time there and no new blood was brought into the breed. The body of the Manx cat has undergone characteristic changes. The rump should be well rounded, being compared to an orange by the British standard. The back is short, the flanks are deep and the long hindlegs are very strong. The skeletal changes led to a loss of the cat's ability to walk gracefully, resulting in the characteristic bobbing, rabbit-like gait known as the 'Manx hop'. Manx cats do not make good tree-climbers, being unable to jump from a great height. The true Manx cats, or 'rumpies', as they are known, have a dimple at the base of the spine, where other cats have their tails. True Manx cats often give birth to dead kittens. This is the reason why the preliminary breeding admits specimens showing a short truncated tail with two to three abbreviated caudal vertebrae. These cats are known as 'stumpies' (2).

Around the year 1970, a longhaired form of the Manx was bred in the United States. The breed is known as the Cymric (3). So far it has remained rather rare, being recognized only by a few American cat fanciers' organizations.

2

Since there is an essential requirement for the specific body type, the coat colour of the Manx is not taken into account by the standard. The Manx is recognized in any colour variety, including Tabby-and-white, which is recognized neither in similarly coloured British Shorthairs nor in any other breed. Similarly, any eye colour matching the overall tone is acceptable. According to the standard, the coat should be soft and double, showing a dense undercoat and an open top coat such as that possessed by a rabbit. The head of the Manx is

3

round and large. The nose should be
longish, without approaching the Persian
type. The cheeks are well developed. The
ears are wide at the base, tapering to
a point.

1

Sphynx (Canadian Hairless)

Hairless cats are said to have been kept by civilizations as ancient as the Aztecs. Specimens are also recorded to have been bred at the beginning of the century in New Mexico, in the United States. They have been described as Mexican Hairless Cats ever since. After a short period of time, however, this breed became extinct.

Since 1966, another breed of hairless cat, which is known as the Sphynx (1), has been bred in the Canadian province of Ontario. These cats are claimed to differ from the Mexican Hairless. They were developed from a hairless mutant of the American Shorthair. In fact, they are not absolutely hairless. They are covered all over with very fine hair. Thin and slightly crimped hair about 1 cm ($\frac{1}{2}$ inch) long (3) is found along the spine, on the legs and on the last few centimetres of the tail; in males also on the testicles. They have no whiskers or eye lashes.

In fact, hairless cats cannot be regarded as a separate breed. The loss of fur can occur with any other breed as a result of a mutation or degeneracy. For example, hairless cats have also cropped up in Rex breeding programmes. Although the Rex is similar in appearance to the Sphynx, the breeds have nothing in common from the point of view of genetics. In spite of the facts mentioned, the Sphynx is considered to be a separate breed, for over the years of breeding, some typical external characteristics have become established. The traits found on the head (2) are: the short nose; the well-developed break and muzzle pinch; the slanting eyes set well back. The relatively short body is set on the thin bow legs. The hindlegs are slightly longer than the forelegs. The Sphynx gives an overall appearance rather similar to that of a Boston Terrier.

The Sphynx has not yet been recognized by many cat associations. At present it is probably most popular with Dutch cat breeders, being bred mostly by people who have developed an allergy to the cat's coat. The early literature often includes reports of hairless cats. They were claimed to have occurred spontaneously in Czechoslovakia and Austria.

3

Hairlessness is genetically determined by a recessive gene. When the deviation is not maintained by deliberate selection, it tends to disappear within a short period of time.

2

1

Japanese Bobtail

In Japan, the Japanese Bobtail (1) has been known for centuries. This fact is corroborated by a great number of ancient paintings and prints. For example, the Gotokuji Temple in Tokyo is decorated with pictures based upon cat themes. The Japanese Bobtail is said to have arrived in Japan from China about 1000 AD. It developed into a separate breed only after the first specimens were brought to the United States in 1968. The breed was standardized there in 1976 and, though not recognized by the FIFe or the GCCF, was accepted and exhibited by the CA in 1986.

The truncated tail is the characteristic feature of the Japanese Bobtail. It is carried curved, so that although its full length is 10—12 cm (4—5 inches) it appears to be shorter. In contrast with the Manx (the two breeds have nothing in common), the Japanese Bobtail exhibits no degeneration or reduction of the caudal vertebrae, but only a considerable abbreviation. The mutation appears in other domestic animals, too. The tail is covered with long hair, which grows in all directions, thus giving an effect rather like a fox's brush or the bobtail of the rabbit. The body of the Japanese Bobtail is sturdy, medium sized and well muscled. The hindlegs are longer than the front, thus being kept bent when the cat is in a standing position. The head (2) of the Japanese Bobtail shows typical characteristics, such as the long and straight nose, high cheek bones and big oval slanting eyes.

1

2

Japanese Bobtails are found in a variety of colours with the rich shades prevailing. The traditional colour combination is the mi-ke or tricolour, consisting of white, black and red. The mi-ke colours can also occur separately or in a bicolour combination (black-and-white, black). Naturally, tortoiseshell Japanese Bobtails are always female. Specimens exhibiting Siamese-type points or ticking are disqualified at shows.

Cats of this breed are highly regarded in Japan, for they are said to bring luck to good people. They have also established themselves as popular family cats.

159

Ruddy Abyssinian

Abyssinians are attractive cats, totally different from the rest of the shorthaired breeds and varieties. The breed was developed by man. Mrs Barrett-Lennard, the wife of a British officer, took care of a cat during her stay in Abyssinia (now Ethiopia). The cat bore a resemblance to the cats depicted on ancient coins, sculpted and painted by the Ancient Egyptians. In 1866, the cat, called Lulu, was brought to Britain by its owner. Over years of careful breeding, the Abyssinian breed developed. In Britain, Abyssinians were recognized as a separate breed in 1882. At the beginning of the century the breed spread all over the world, being most widely bred in the United States today.

The agouti-ticking of the Abyssinian's coat is a distinctive feature of the breed. Each hair has two to three dark-coloured bands, as already described under the semi-longhair Somali breed. The ticked hair is evenly distributed all over the body. There should be no markings or patches on the coat. The belly and the inside of the legs are covered with paler hair without the ticking. The dark line running down the Abyssinian's back up to the top of the tail is tolerated by the standard providing it is not too wide.

3

According to basic coat colours, Abyssinians are divided into several colour varieties. Eight varieties are recognized by the standard. The Ruddy Abyssinian (1, 2) shows black ticking on warm brown ground, just like the fur of a hare or rabbit. The brick red nose is rimmed with black and the paw pads (3) are black. (For a description of the Sorrel — alternatively known as Russet or Cinnamon — Abyssinian and the Blue Abyssinian see page 162.) Finally, the coat of the Beige Fawn (also known as Cream) Abyssinian is a dull beige with dark cream agouti-ticking. The nose tip should be pink, outlined in shell, and the paw pads should be shell.

Abyssinians are graceful in their appearance and movements, and are rather cautious in their behaviour. An unknown object is first carefully examined with paws and only then sniffed. Abyssinians are devoted to their masters, with a reputation as affectionate companions. Although unobtrusive, they enjoy being stroked. They are not keen to live in large cat groups. Their voice is quiet, even when they are on heat. They make good climbers.

2

1

Sorrel Abyssinian

The Abyssinian has a flexible and firm body of medium size and length, which is set high on fairly slender legs. The tail is quite long, and it is thicker at the base, narrowing to the slim tip. The wedge-shaped head is of medium size, but it is shorter and less pointed than in the Siamese. The medium-length nose should be slightly curved, neither with a break nor straight in profile. The nose tip is rimmed with a dark colour corresponding to the ground colour. The almond-shaped eyes are large and striking and may be either green or amber. They should be outlined in the same colour as the nose tip. It is claimed by experienced breeders of Abyssinians that the eye colour frequently changes in accordance with the animal's mood or health condition. The ears are rather conspicuous, and are largish and set wide apart. They appear attentively pricked, being pointed at the tips. Abyssinians often show characteristic ear tufts resembling those of the lynx. Recently the following four silver varieties have been recognized: Silver Ruddy, Silver Sorrel, Silver Blue and Silver Beige Fawn.

3

The Sorrel Abyssinian (1) has a coppery red coat with each hair ticked red-brown. The paw pads (3) are pink, as is the nose tip which should be outlined in red-brown. The blue-grey coat of the Blue Abyssinian (2) is ticked with a steel-blue colour. The brick red muzzle is blue rimmed, and the pads are blue-grey.

The kittens are born rather dark. The ticking does not show until the kitten is about two months old, first appearing on the tail and legs. Litters average between two and four. The kittens are slow to develop, though not so slow as the Somali. Abyssinians and Somalis are regarded as a single breed. Although the reason is unknown, more male Abyssinians than females are born. The ruddy colouring is genetically dominant. The sorrel kitten is only produced where both parents carry the allele determining red colour, although their actual colour is ruddy.

2

1

Cornish Rex

The curly-coated cat is a mutant of a common shorthaired cat. It was first reported in East Prussia during the 1930s. In 1947, a similar specimen was found near a hospital in East Berlin. Neither of the two was recognized by breeders, and in fact curly-coated cats were first developed by Cornish breeders. In 1950, a Mrs Enninsmore discovered a curly-coated male kitten in the litter of a tortie-and-white cat. The kitten was named Kallibunker. The owner consulted a famous cat fancier and rabbit breeder and more curly-coated kittens were produced by back-crossing; the breed was named the Rex, after the similar mutation in rabbits. As Kallibunker was born in Cornwall, England, the breed is known today as the Cornish Rex (1). Since 1967, Rex cats have been recognized as a separate breed in Britain as well as on the Continent.

The coat of the Cornish Rex is short and dense. It has a plushy, almost silky texture without any guard hairs. The length of awn and down hairs is about half that of normal shorthaired cats. The hairs are rather crimped or curly (4), particularly on the back and tail, thus giving the appearance of a fresh perm. The whiskers and eyebrows are curled, though retaining their normal length. The body of the Cornish Rex should be sturdy and muscular, with long, thin legs. The head (3) is wedge-shaped, with a longish nose and strong chin. The flat forehead is slanted backward so that in profile an almost straight line is seen from its centre to the tip of the nose. The ears are set high on the head, being rather wide at the base.

3

More specimens were produced by mating the German Rex to the Cornish Rex, proving that the mutations, both English and German, are either genetically identical or closely related. According to the revised standard, each type has been regarded as a separate breed since 1982 probably due to the different structure of the body and head. Mutual mating is therefore no longer

desirable. The head of the German Rex is more rounded, showing a less distinct break. In comparison with the Cornish Rex, the body of the German Rex (2) is more robust, showing a broader chest, just like that of the European Shorthair.

2

4

1

Devon Rex

In 1960, a curly-coated male kitten was discovered by a Miss Beryl Cox in Buckfastleigh, Devon. The kitten was named Kirlee. Kirlee and its offspring were mated to the Cornish Rex specimens. The crossing resulted only in plain-coated kittens. It was obvious that the two represent unrelated mutations which are determined by different genes. Curly kittens were produced neither from matings to the German Rex nor to cats of the Rex type, which meanwhile appeared in Oregon and Ohio, in the United States. The more recent variety has been described as the Devon Rex (1, 2). It differs from the Cornish Rex in external appearance, and it was therefore decided not to mate the Devon Rex to the Cornish Rex so as to preserve the typical traits of each variety.

The coat (4) of the Devon Rex is of the same soft texture as that of the Cornish Rex, showing the slightly modified guard hairs. The coat is less curled than that of the Cornish Rex, however, the whiskers and eyebrows being crinkled and of medium or short length. The Devon Rex is also distinguished by the body build and head type. The body is muscular and broad-chested. The bow legs are quite short. The head (3) is a short wedge, resembling the head of the Burmese. There should be protruding cheek bones and full cheeks in addition to a strongly marked break to the short nose. The large ears are set rather far forward. The ear tips are rounded, showing distinct ear tufts, which are slightly shorter than those of the lynx.

3

Due to the modified structure of the coat, Rex cats are less resistant to changes in environment. It is therefore recommended that breeders counteract possible drops in temperature by boosting the intake of fats. On the other hand, Rex cats are more resistant to diseases than any other breed.

It is quite easy to prepare the coat for a show. As the fine hair can be damaged by combing or grooming, all that is needed before judging is hand-grooming.

Brown Burmese

The Burmese should by no means be mistaken for the Birman, as there are essential differences between the two. Burmese are short-hairs of uniform colours, while the Birman (or the Sacred Cat of Burma) is a semi-longhair exhibiting points colours and white gloves on the paws. Burmese cats, or at least cats closely related to the breed or similar in appearance, have been known in the Far East for a great many years. Just like the Korat, a cat closely resembling the Burmese is depicted in the ancient Cat-Book Poems. The depictions are considered to be early examples of Havana Browns or Burmese. The cat was known as the Supalak or Thong Daeng. According to more recent Oriental literary works, the cat used to be kept in all wealthy houses and temples, as it was claimed to bring luck and fortune.

In 1930, a walnut-brown female hybrid named Wong Mau was taken from Rangoon in Burma to California by the retired US Navy psychiatrist Dr Joseph C. Thompson. As the cat was originally regarded as a Siamese of a different colour, it was mated to a Seal Point Siamese male. The crossing resulted in Siamese-like kittens. However, crosses between the offspring produced the first true Burmese cats. The breeding experiments led to the establishment of the Burmese breed, which was given official recognition in 1936. At that time, Burmese were only found in their basic brown coat colour.

2

The Brown Burmese (1), also known as the Sable Burmese, has a seal brown coat, nose and paw pads. A dark brown coat, bordering on black, is regarded as a fault.

The overall tone of Brown Burmese kittens (2) differs a great deal from that of adult animals. Their coat is much lighter. The face sometimes shows hints of points colours, shading or faint tabby markings. However, all imperfections disappear at maturity, at about 15 months of age.

1

Blue Burmese

In 1947, the first Brown Burmese specimens (see page 168) were brought to Great Britain. After several years of breeding, a Blue Burmese (1) was produced in 1955. The success stimulated further experiments, resulting in new colour varieties which have been bred up to the present day. Blue Burmese have a blue-grey coat with a light silvery sheen on the ears, face and paws. The muzzle and paw pads are of the same colour shade. The blue of the Burmese is much lighter than the blue-grey colouring of Russian and British Blues.

The kittens of the Blue Burmese are much paler than adults. They show a distinct dark-coloured mask and, sometimes, tabby markings on the back. Both imperfections disappear at maturity.

2

Experienced cat fanciers will know that blue is among the most common of colour varieties. The Blue Longhair (Persian) is easily distinguished from the other blues. It is much more complicated to distinguish between shorthaired blues. There are eight blue varieties, the representatives of respective breeds differing mainly in the head type, as can be clearly seen on the following schematic pictures: the Blue Burmese (2), the Chartreux (3), the Russian Blue (4), the British Blue (5), the Blue European Shorthair (6), the Korat (7) and the Foreign Blue (8). Apart from the colour varieties listed, blue specimens of other breeds can occur, such as the three Rex breeds and the Manx. In these particular cases, more striking characteristics than the head type serve the purpose of classification.

3

4

5

6

7

8

1

Chocolate Burmese

Like many other breeds, Burmese occur in a variety of colours. The other colour varieties have developed from the original brown colouring. In the United States, from where the Burmese have spread worldwide, the original Brown Burmese is the only variety regarded as the true Burmese. The other varieties are classified under the breed name Malayan, however. The breed name has not become established in other countries. The current FIFe standards recognize an overall number of ten varieties, but there are a few specimens of more recent varieties which have not yet been recognized.

Although having a common origin (as mentioned on page 168), the look of Burmese cats indicates that the appearance of the early specimens differed in minor details, for they were bred in different parts of the world. For example, the eye shape is specified as round by the American standard, while the British and European standards call for eyes of a more oval shape.

2

1

The Chocolate Burmese (1) is also described as the Champagne Burmese. The colour of the muzzle and paw pads should be a warm milk chocolate as should the overall coat colour. The fur on the head, particularly on the mask, may be slightly darker. The paw pads sometimes shade into cinnamon.

The kittens (2) of Chocolate Burmese cats are born almost white. A kitten cannot be classified in its proper colour until it is several weeks old. As with the Siamese, kittens first get the proper coat around the muzzle and on the paw pads.

Lilac Burmese

As with other breeds, the head of the Burmese shows many typical traits. The head should be slightly rounded in profile and frontal views, with good breadth between the ears, having a strong chin and full cheeks and tapering to a short and blunt edge. A muzzle pinch is a definite fault. The medium-sized ears should be broad at the base, with slightly rounded tips. They are set wide apart and have a slight forward tilt. The outer line of the ears is continuous with the upper part of the face. This does not apply to males which develop a typical, more robust skull shape with full cheeks as secondary sexual characteristics. The nose should be short and broad, with a distinct break, which should neither be too deep nor have an indentation. In profile, the chin should show a strong lower jaw. The eyes should be set well apart by a distance which should be larger than the width of the eye. They should be large and lustrous, the top line of the eyes showing an Oriental slant towards the nose, the lower line being rounded. The eye colour is yellow; golden-yellow being the most desirable shade. Any shade of pure yellow is acceptable, amber included. Copper or green-yellow eyes are a fault. A slight greenish hue is tolerated in some colour varieties of the Burmese, but such an animal is not eligible for championship status. In judging, animals with clear blue eyes are disqualified.

The Lilac Burmese (1, 2) is also known as the Platinum Burmese. Its coat should be dove-grey with a slightly pinkish cast. The Lilac Burmese is in fact much paler than its Persian equivalent. The muzzle and foot pads are lavender, with a fine pink hue. The kittens of the Lilac Burmese are born almost white, as are those of the Chocolate Burmese (see page 172). Lilac Burmese were rare until quite recently, but are now much more commonly seen at shows.

2

1

Red Burmese

The following two varieties, the Red Burmese (1) and the Cream Burmese (see page 178), show only minor differences in the overall tone and the colour of the foot pads. The coat of an adult Red Burmese should be a warm orange colour, just like a pale tangerine. Cream Burmese have a pastel cream coat. Both varieties usually exhibit an uneven tone and slight tabby barrings. These are permitted if the cat is otherwise perfect in all respects. As with the equivalent varieties of other breeds, red and cream colours are almost invariably accompanied by tabby barrings or marbling of variable intensity. Pigmented patches on the muzzle and foot pads are regarded as imperfections.

The first Red Burmese cats were obtained by deliberate crossbreeding between the Blue Burmese female and the Red Tabby British Shorthair or Red Point Siamese male. A large number of inappropriate hybrids were produced at the very beginning of the programme. Although the results of the breeding were at first disappointing, breeders eventually succeeded in incorporating the red gene into the Burmese breed. The prerequisites for success were, as with other breeding experiments, a mixture of good fortune and perseverance.

2

It is rather difficult to classify the new-born Red and Cream kittens (2) into their correct colour varieties (as already mentioned with the Chocolate and Lilac Burmese). The actual colour cannot be determined until about six weeks of age.

1

Cream Burmese

The body of the Burmese shows a number of typical traits. It is of medium length and size although it looks much more delicate at first glance. The chest of the Burmese is strong and massive, and should be rounded in profile. The back should be straight, and almost horizontal from shoulder to rump. The legs are quite slender, giving a rather delicate appearance. The hindlegs are slightly longer than the forelegs. The paws are neat and oval in shape, being much more rounded than those of the Siamese. The tail is straight, not too thick at the base and of medium length. It is shorter than in Siamese and longer than in longhairs (Persians), tapering only slightly to a rounded tip.

Any suggestion of either the lithe Siamese type, or the cobbiness of the British European Shorthair is considered a fault at shows. Judges usually select against such specimens, thus helping to preserve the Burmese of the desired type. The characteristic elegance of these cats gives a rather exotic impression.

2

1

The cream variety (1) is quite common among Burmese. The coat is a pastel cream, the nose tip and paw pads are pink. No pigmented patches should be found on the mask and muzzle, as with the Red Burmese.

The Burmese bear on average five to seven kittens, the litters being larger than with any other breed. The new-born kittens (2) are pale, and it would take a long time for a breeder to assess the kitten's colour potential were it not for the paw pads and the muzzle, which usually take on the proper colour earlier than the coat. Nevertheless, with some varieties it is rather difficult to tell the actual colour, even in adults. This applies to the Chocolate, Lilac, Red and Cream Burmese.

Brown Tortie Burmese

Apart from the Cream Burmese described on page 178 there are four recognized tortoiseshell varieties. The Brown Tortie Burmese (1, 2) is the basic variety. All tortoiseshell varieties are based on the same coat pattern, which is simple and easily derivable. The Brown Tortie Burmese is, as its name suggests, brown, displaying numerous cream blotches of moderate size, which should be evenly distributed. The same principle applies to the other tortoiseshell varieties. The Blue Tortie Burmese is pale blue with cream patches, the Chocolate Tortie Burmese is a mixture of a milk chocolate colour and pale cream, and the Lilac Tortie (Lilac Cream) Burmese displays a lilac-and-cream coat. The colour should be evenly distributed all over the body, legs and tail. The colour of the muzzle and paw pads (3) should match the overall tone of the Brown Tortie Burmese.

As with other breeds, Tortoiseshell Burmese are always female. This is because the gene determining red colour is linked with the sex chromosome X.

Tortoiseshell Burmese cats have been recognized by the FIFe since 1983. At that time, the coat colour was not considered so important in judging at shows as was the adherence to the type in

1

2

3

conformation and overall appearance.
Nowadays, Tortoiseshell Burmese are
assessed by the same standard as the
other colour varieties.

Chocolate Tortie Burmese

So far, there are only a few Chocolate Tortie Burmese (1) in existence, but thanks to their interesting appearance (a milk chocolate coloured coat with creamy patches) it might soon be more widely spread. All chocolate-coloured cats or those with a chocolate element in their coat are nowadays very popular with the breeders.

As well as the ten varieties of Burmese so far recognized there have been other colour varieties developed all over the world. Most of these probably originate in Great Britain, where the GCCF recognizes several other colour combinations. The Burmese is perhaps most popular in New Zealand and Australia, where apart from the standard varieties the White Burmese is also widely spread. Another colour variety is the Black Burmese (2), which has been recognized in the United States as the 'Bombay' since 1976. It was the result of a mating between a Brown Burmese female and a Black American Shorthair male in 1958. Bombays are of medium size, with a black muzzle and brilliant yellow-brown eyes. Most characteristic is their black coat with a glossy shine, which reminds many of patent leather. These cats are sometimes referred to as mini-panthers, for they are similar in appearance to the black leopard of India. So far they have not been recognized outside the United States.

Burmese with remarkably longer hair have also been bred in the United States. These cats were called Tiffanies because of the resemblance between their coat and tiffany material. Currently they are few in number but when they become more widespread and are recognized, they will probably be classed with the semi-longhairs, as is the case with the Somali.

Burmese cats are a good example of how isolated breeding programmes pursued in different parts of the world can result in the differential development of various parts of a cat's body. Nor does it take long for the departure to develop. For example, American Burmese cats differ slightly from those originating mostly in

2

Great Britain not only in their
conformation, but also in the shape of the
head, eyes and ears. The respective
European and North American standards
differ accordingly.

1

Lilac Tortie Burmese

The coat of this particular variety (1) should be a mixture of lilac and light cream. The coat of Burmese cats should be very short, close-lying and dense, free of an undercoat, and with a fine satin-like texture. The hairs should be evenly pigmented all over. Almost all colour varieties of Burmese cats display a paler shade when compared with their equivalent varieties in other breeds. This applies especially to the blue, red and cream varieties. Furthermore, the colour shades into a slightly paler tone on the underparts and chest. The mask and ears on the other hand may be slightly darker, reminding us of the distant relationship with the Siamese (Burmese cats were mated with Siamese at the very beginning of the breeding programme.) As with the Siamese, any shading on the back is considered a great fault. A few white hairs will be tolerated in judging if the animal is otherwise excellent. Any hair of the wrong colour should not occur in large amounts or form white patches.

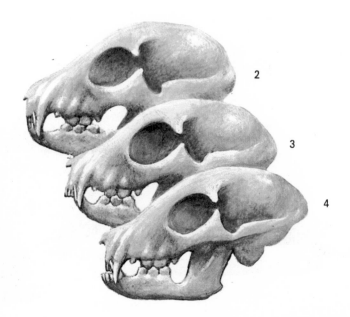

2

3

4

A malformation of the dentition is one of the many symptoms of degeneration which may appear as a result of inbreeding. These changes may also be found more often in Burmese, for the early specimens were produced by backcrossing. On the other hand, inbreeding may improve other traits which have not yet become genetically well established. A normal, healthy cat shows a correct bite. This means that the upper and lower incisors meet correctly (2). As a consequence of degeneration, the upper incisors may project over the lower. This is known as an overshot jaw, or overbite (3). When the lower front teeth protrude, the malformation is referred to as an undershot jaw , or underbite (4). In judging, both overbite and underbite are penalized as imperfections in the overall appearance of the head. Nowadays, they are regarded as faults only when the departure from the normal is more than 2 mm ($\frac{1}{16}$ inch). This is because such deviations often result in a disproportionate head shape. In cases where the underbite is severe, the cat's tongue may also protrude.

1

Blue Tortie Burmese

In spite of being known for quite a long time, the Blue Tortie Burmese (1, 2) has not yet become widely spread. In the original standard for the variety it used to be described as the Blue Cream Burmese. The current standard came into force in 1983. Although the name was altered, the requirements have remained practically the same (a light blue colour mixed with pale cream patches of moderate size). The only difference is found in the intensity of the colours.

As regards the temperament of Burmese cats, they have independent personalities and are individualists even among cats. As well as possessing all the general feline attributes, Burmese cats are very intelligent and affectionate. They usually become completely devoted to one person, although they are friendly with the other members of the family as well. They can be bred in groups, coping well with restricted spaces. They enjoy the company of other domestic animals, for example dogs. Burmese cats are good-natured, humorous and playful until quite old. They often live to the age of 16 to 19 years. They are not very noisy, being more highly vocal only when on heat, though less so than Siamese. Burmese cats are unusually adaptable and well-suited for life in city apartments and flats, for they do not scratch the curtains and furniture with their claws provided they are given an appropriate scratching post.

The coat of the Burmese requires no special care. After grooming, the coat should be slightly smoothed with a moist piece of cloth to remove the rest of the dead hairs. Particular care should be given to the eyes of Burmese cats, as some, particularly pale specimens, may show some tear staining around the eyes.

2

1

Russian Blue

Russian Blues (1) first appeared at shows as early as 1880 in London. Their origin, however, remains unknown. A number of amber-eyed blue cats are said to have been brought from the Russian port of Archangel to Britain after the year 1883. This is why the breed used to be known as the Archangel Cat.

The original Russian Blues were more robust than recent specimens. It was not until after World War II that British and Scandinavian breeders crossed Russian Blues with Blue Point Siamese in order to produce a slimmer body type. The type was specified by the standard in 1965. The standard calls for a cat with a svelte and graceful body, and a medium-strong bone structure. The tail is fairly long, tapering to a point. At first sight the Russian Blue seems to bear a resemblance to the Chartreux, but the blue colour of the coat is the only trait they share. The quality of the coat is, however, rather different. The coat of the Russian Blue is short, thick, plushy and upstanding — like the coat of a seal. There should be a slight silvery sheen. The Russian Blue also differs from the British Shorthair in the head type (2). The head is a short flat wedge, with the forehead long, straight or slightly bulging. The whisker pads are prominent. The eyes are almond-shaped and set rather wide apart. They should be a vivid green colour. The ears are large and pointed, wide at the base and set apart, vertically to the head. A particular characteristic of the breed is the thinness of the skin of the ears. It should be nearly transparent.

Russian Blues are only affectionate to those they know, being quite shy with other people. Adult animals are gentle and rather pensive. They adapt well, easily becoming accustomed to life in city apartments. In contrast with the vocal Siamese, Russian Blues tend to be quiet, even when they are on heat.

The coat of the Russian Blue requires special treatment. Because of the upstanding fur, care must be taken not to polish it. Therefore, the coat should first be brushed against the direction of growth and only then gently combed back in the natural direction. Grooming powder, if used, should be of a coarse texture so as not to make the coat too soft.

188

2

1

Korat

The Korat (1) is one of the oldest breeds of shorthaired cats of the semi-oriental type. The breed derives its name from Korat, the north-eastern province of Thailand, where it is most widely spread. These cats are known there as the Si-Sawat. The breed is described in the Smud Koi Parchment (Cat-Book Poems), which is deposited in the Thai National Library in Bangkok. The manuscript dates from 1350—1767, the reign of the Siamese dynasty of Ayudhya. The Korat is described there as having a 'smooth coat with roots like clouds and tips like silver and the eyes shining like dew drops on the lotus leaf'. This is a brief description, yet it comes near the truth, as the colour of the Korat's coat is actually blue with a distinct silver sheen. This results from light reflected from the fine hairs in the outer coat. The fur is very thick, perhaps the thickest of all feline breeds. It is glossy, fine and close-lying. The head shape (2) is another particular characteristic of the Korat. It is of medium size and distinctly heart-shaped. The face is heart-shaped as well. The eyes are rather large and round, preferably deep green in colour. The ears are also large and round, and wide at the base. The nose of the Korat resembles that of the lion, being shorter in comparison with the Russian Blue. The tail is heavy at the base, tapering to a point.

The Korat has remained a natural breed, outcrossing to other breeds being forbidden. Korats have a reputation for being hyper-sensitive to certain substances, particularly sedatives and anaesthetics. The dose which usually acts upon cats of other breeds for a few hours is enough to affect the Korat for as long as three days. Korats do not tolerate certain antibiotics either.

2

1

Litters of Korats are not very large, containing on average three to four kittens. In young kittens, faint tabby markings can often be seen in the coat, but these tend to disappear within a short period of time. The blue eyes take on the proper green colour rather late, at about three or even four years of age. Unless the kittens become accustomed to human company by the time they are three to five weeks of age, they grow wild and untamable. However, once accustomed to humans, they make devoted pets. Korats are said to be happiest when they are the only pets in the family, for they do not want to share human affection with other cats. Korats retain their playfulness up to old age.

Seal Point Siamese

Siamese are prized above all for their colouring. This consists of the body colour of the coat contrasting with the points colours on the face, ears, legs and tail. The English names of colour varieties became established during early years of the breed and have been used throughout the world ever since.

The early Siamese (2, 3) bred at the turn of the century looked very different from the breed as we know it today. They bore a considerable resemblance to modern British Shorthairs in body and head type. The body was more robust, with the head sturdy and broad. Both characteristics would have been regarded as faults by current standards. In the early 1920s, breeders decided to develop a breed which would show a radical difference in shape when compared with the early Siamese cats. In the first place they focused upon changes in the overall appearance of the body and head. Other traits were also taken into consideration, namely those regarded as abnormalities or signs of degeneration. This applies to the degenerative changes in the tail, which used to be stumpy, twisted or kinked in many early Siamese.

The Seal Point Siamese (1) was at first the only variety to be recognized, being the most widely spread as well as the most attractive, due to its dramatic contrast. The brown colour at the points reminds many of seal skin, hence the name of the

3

variety. The body colour is cream (fawn), shading into a darker colour on the back. The muzzle is a seal brown and so are the paw pads.

2

1

Blue Point Siamese

Siamese of the modern type should be cats of medium size with a longish, svelte body, which should be well-proportioned as regards the bone and muscular structure. The legs of the Siamese should be long and slim, and the hindlegs should be slightly longer than the front ones so that the body is slightly elevated towards the tail. The paws are small and neat, and oval in shape. The longer the tail the better; it should be thin at the base, tapering to a point. A heavy or thick tail, even if only at the base, is considered a fault. Consequently, animals showing kinked tails or other caudal malformations (3) should not be selected for further breeding.

The elongated head is of medium size. The skull is slightly arching in profile. The forehead should narrow in a straight line without a break to a fine muzzle (2). The ears are large and broad, set wide apart at the base. In a pricked position, the outer edges of the ears should form a straight line with the contours of the head. Strongly developed cheeks as well as a muzzle pinch are undesirable, since they can distort the straight line of the wedge. The lustrous, deep-blue eyes are almond-shaped, set wide apart and slanting towards the nose. The coat is short, glossy and fine in quality and perfectly close-lying.

Blue Point Siamese (1) result from the action of the gene determining the dilution of black colour (which is in fact dark brown in the Siamese) to blue. Blue Points are quite common today. The body colour should be a glacial white shading into light blue. It tones in with the

3

distinct grey-blue points, which should be
a cold colour. Blue Points were first
recorded in 1894 in Great Britain,
receiving official recognition as
a separate colour variety only in 1936.

2

1

Chocolate Point Siamese

There is total number of 18 colour varieties, colour combinations and pattern types in Siamese cats. Seal Points were the first Siamese to be recognized (see page 192). By incorporating appropriate genes, the other varieties were derived — such as the Chocolate Point, which is one of the earliest-known varieties. The body colour of the Chocolate Point Siamese (1, 2) is an ivory white. The points, muzzle and paw pads are a milk chocolate. Chocolate Points are frequently mistaken for Seal Points. Originally they were classed as poorly coloured Seal Points. They were standardized as a separate variety only in 1949 in Europe. The difference in the colour of the paw pads between the two varieties is clearly seen in the pictures — the Seal Point (3) and the Chocolate Point (4).

A slight shading of the coat is acceptable on the sides, providing it corresponds to the particular points colour. The coat can be slightly darker in the centre of the back. The underparts should be paler, nearly white. A dark smudge on the belly is a definite fault (though it was frequently found in the early Siamese). The body colour is always dependent upon the colour of the points. The Lilac Point, for example, has a bluish white coat with a pinkish tone, while the coat of the Chocolate Point is a warm ivory white shade.

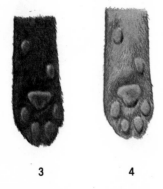

3   4

Siamese were once much more popular than they are today. Great numbers of them used to compete at shows, especially Seal Points and Chocolate Points.

2

1

Lilac Point Siamese

At first glance, Siamese can be identified by their striking colouring and svelte body type. The body type is actually rare among cats, being typical only of Siamese and Oriental Shorthairs. Points colours are restricted to the face, ears, legs and tail, for these parts of the body are less supplied with blood and are thus cooler. Therefore, due to processes taking place in the skin, larger amounts of pigment are stored in the hairs at the points. The dark-coloured areas can also appear on the other parts of the body where the coat has moulted, in places where the bald patches are exposed to low temperatures. Animals reared in cool environments or those allowed to go outdoors in winter commonly develop darker coats than those brought up in warm homes. These usually have short, pale and far less dense coats.

All varieties of Siamese should have brilliant deep blue eyes (4) slanting towards the nose and set wide apart. The early Siamese had mostly light blue eyes (5). Siamese with light blue eyes still occur from time to time. This means that the dark blue colour has not yet become genetically well established. Such specimens are less valued by breeders, though otherwise excellent in other respects. Siamese frequently develop a squint (6), either in one or both eyes. This is great fault which is easily passed on to the progeny. Breeders invariably select against squint-eyed animals, yet sometimes the squint may only be temporary. The temporary squint may be caused by excitement at a show or by an illness.

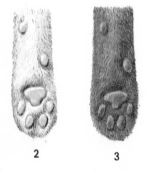

2   3

Lilac Point Siamese (1) have a bluish white coat with a pinkish tint, the points being a greyish pink. Both colours should be a cold shade. Thus, the variety is

198

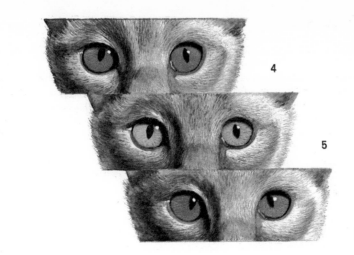

4

5

6

sometimes referred to as the Frost Point Siamese. Animals showing a blue shade at the points look more like poorly coloured Blue Points. The colour of the muzzle and foot pads is the most distinctive feature, being lavender-pink in Lilac Points (2) and blue-grey in Blue Points (3).

1

Red Point Siamese

The precise origin of the Siamese remains unknown. Specialists are in agreement that the breed originates somewhere in the Far East, either in Thailand (formerly Siam) or in some neighbouring country. The Bengal cat (*Prionailurus bengalensis*, 3) may be one of its ancestors. It is a common wild cat in the region. The species occasionally inter-breeds with domestic cats, just like the European Wild Cat in Central Europe does. The theory is corroborated with common develop-mental traits as well as with the resemblance the Siamese bears to the Bengal cat.

The first specimens of Siamese cats in Britain, the male Pho and the female Mia, were brought here in 1884 by Owen Gould, the British Consul General in Bangkok. The cats were given to him by Pradganipoh, the King of Siam. The first Siamese were exhibited at the Crystal Palace, London, in 1890 by the consul's sister. The first standard of points laid down for the Siamese was published on *Our Cats* magazine in 1892.

However, Siamese cats are reported to have occurred much earlier. There is an evidence that they had been kept in Ayudhya, the ancient capital of Siam, which was founded in 1350 and was burnt down by the Burmese in 1767. The Cat-Book Poems (dating back to that time) present a beautiful depiction of the Siamese along with the Korat and Burmese. The German explorer Peter Simon Pallas gives us another description. In his travels published in 1793, he described a cat he had seen around the Caspian Sea, which was very similar in appearance to the Siamese.

3

The Red Point Siamese (1, 2) evolved from the Tortie Point Siamese around the year 1960. It was recognized as a separate variety in 1966. The body colour of the coat is off-white, slightly shading into cream. The muzzle and paw pads are pink. Red Points are usually males.

2

1

Cream Point Siamese

On the North American continent, only the varieties with basic points colours (seal, blue, chocolate and lilac) are regarded as true Siamese, the other varieties being termed Colourpoint Shorthairs. The difference is regarded as of paramount importance and, as a result, breeding between the two colour groupings is banned by some cat fanciers' associations in the United States. The Albino Siamese was developed by American breeders. As it has no points, it bears a close resemblance to the Oriental White. The cat known as the shi-mi is said to be kept in Tibetan temples. It looks like a Siamese with jet black points.

The Tonkinese (2) is another variety which was developed some 30 years ago in Canada. It is a hybrid of the Siamese and Burmese. Their mating results in split characteristics, the litter consisting of a quarter Siamese, a quarter Burmese and a half Tonkinese progeny. The Tonkinese cannot be recognized as a separate breed or variety, as its progeny would always split into the two original breeds and only half would show the particular hybrid characteristics. Tonkinese are bred in four colours, which correspond to the four basic colours of the original breeds: natural mink, honey mink, champagne and blue (blue-grey).

2

1

The Cream Point Siamese (1) has only
been standardized since 1973. As with
other breeds, cream colour resulted from
the action of a dilute gene upon red
colour. It has so far remained a rarity at
shows. The coat is a cream white, the
points are a pastel cream shade. The
muzzle and paw pads are pink.

Tortie Point Siamese

Although Siamese cats with multicoloured points have been known for many years, a new classification for them has only been in force since 1980. They were classified as Tortie Points, Tabby (Lynx) Points and Tabby Tortie (Patched Tabby; Torbie) Points. Each group can be subdivided according to the prevailing colour — seal, blue (2), chocolate or lilac.

The four varieties of Tortie Point Siamese have been known since 1952. In recent years, they have been more widely exhibited at shows. The body colour of the coat as well as the colouring of the muzzle and paw pads (3) can be seal, blue, chocolate or lilac. The points are patched with colours corresponding to the basic colour variety (Seal Tortie Point, 1). As with the other breeds, red colour at the points is determined by the female sex and therefore the Tortie Points are female-only varieties.

It is not only their elegant, svelte body which has gained the breed its popularity. Siamese are also extraordinarily devoted to man. They have a character which sets them apart. Siamese not only demand attention, they compel it from their owners all the time. They hate to stay alone, being jealous of both other cats and humans. Although Siamese enjoy the company of other cats, they prefer to stay with humans. They are unusually vocal, commonly responding to the human voice. They are also highly intelligent. Siamese cats take easily to a lead or collar and therefore can learn to be walked like dogs.

3

Siamese are rather prolific animals, their litters often being larger than those of the other breeds. They are rather precocious, maturing as early as about five months old. When in season Siamese, males in particular, call in a penetrating, almost harsh voice. The early Siamese used to have a more melodious voice than the recent type with its elongated wedge-

1

shaped head. The altered voice is
obviously connected with the difference
in the anatomical structure of the head
and vocal cords.

2

Tabby Point Siamese (Lynx Point Siamese)

The eight varieties of Tabby Point Siamese fully correspond to the equivalent varieties without tabby markings at the points. Red and Cream Points constitute the only exception, as tabby markings at the points are to be found in all animals. Such specimens are acceptable at shows and therefore no special standard has been devised for red and cream specimens with tabby points. Before 1983, breeders used to select against specimens with prominent tabby markings. Such animals were generally considered to be 'wrongly' coloured, as tabby markings are a dominant trait which is passed on to the progeny and which becomes manifest in generations to come.

The body colour of the coat should be as pale as possible, preferably free of any shading. The mask, however, should have clear tabby stripes (2), especially around the eyes and nose, with black or dark rimming or toning to match the points on the eyelids. The tail should have clearly defined rings and end in a solid tip colour.

It is rather difficult to classify each of the four Tabby Tortie Points into its proper colour variety. Apart from the tabby barrings, the points should be mottled (prominent tabby stripes are paid greater attention in judging than the quality of the mottling). Respective varieties are best identified by the colour of the paw pads and muzzle. Seal and Blue Points (1) are the only common varieties. The paw pads of the Blue Tabby Point Siamese are blue-grey (3).

3

Siamese kittens are a very light colour when born; the first hint of points colour does not begin to appear until two weeks of age (kittens reared in a warm environment may show it later). The proper points colour first appears on the nose and ear flaps. A kitten can only be

2

classified within its proper colour variety
when about four to six weeks old. Soon
after birth, the breeder can only guess the
colour variety by the colour of the muzzle
and paw pads. The full colour appears
only when the cat is nearly one year old.
A slightly crimped coat in some kittens
may also show faint tabby stripes and
rings on the tail. Both imperfections
usually disappear as the kittens mature.

1

Oriental White (Foreign White)

The body type of the Oriental Shorthair (the group to which the Oriental White belongs) is identical to that of the Siamese and therefore the two are regarded as a single breed. Oriental Shorthairs differ from Siamese only in their colour, which is solid without points. (They were once called Siamese without points.) As they were produced by crossbreeding British Shorthairs to Siamese, they are to be found in the same varieties as British Shorthairs. Tipped and bicoloured Oriental Shorthairs are the only varieties which have not yet been recognized. Their standardization is, however, only a question of time, for they have already been accepted for competition. Being analogous to the Chocolate Point Siamese, the Oriental Cinnamon has not yet been recognized by the standard either.

The coat colour of the Oriental White (1, 2) should be pure white without shading into any other colour, yellow in particular. The paw pads (3) and muzzle are pink. Oriental Whites are the only Oriental Shorthairs with clear, brilliant blue eyes. Breeders select against odd-eyed Oriental Whites, as well as against specimens in which the white coat colour is linked with deafness and where females bear kittens with blackish smudges on their heads. Before starting a new breeding programme in 1962, British breeders classified all the characteristics mentioned as undesirable. Thanks to consistent selective breeding, the defects no longer manifest themselves in the breed.

Apart from the males of the same variety, Oriental White females can be mated to Siamese (except for Red and Cream Points) in order to maintain or improve the quality of the beautiful blue eyes. However, the litter may contain kittens of other Siamese and Oriental varieties, since an Oriental White female almost invariably carries undetected genes for other colours than white. The inheritance of colours in Oriental Whites is governed by the same laws as for other cats.

3

208

1

2

Oriental Blue

Oriental Shorthairs are a very promising breed as they meet the top requirements of most breeders of pedigree cats. They have an elegant body, lively and endearing character and are easy to breed. They have been developed only recently, receiving recognition as late as 1974, with the exception of the Havana (see page 218), which had been recognized and classified as a separate breed earlier. (It should be noted that a Professor Schwangart of Dresden developed a similar breed of lissom cats in black and blue varieties. They used to be referred to as cats of Egyptian type. Unfortunately, the results of his many years work were completely destroyed during World War II.)

As with many other breeds, Oriental Shorthairs are recognized in a blue variety. The prominent characteristic of Oriental Shorthairs — the slender body — should be particularly well-developed in Oriental Blues (1). The coat colour of the Oriental Blue is a light blue with a beautiful sheen. The muzzle and paw pads are a slate blue-grey. The eyes should be deep green without any suggestion of yellow, as with the other varieties of Oriental Shorthairs (except for Oriental Whites). Apart from the green, only American standards permit amber eye colour as well.

The Oriental head type (2), identical to that of Siamese cats, is unique among the pedigree feline breeds. As the breed has been developed only recently, cats with a new, modern head type were used for mating. Consequently, no specimens with the 'old-fashioned' head type are to be found among Oriental Shorthairs. This has proved to be to breeders' advantage, for no other type would interfere with the proper breed, unless it crops up by a mistake on the part of the breeder.

2

1

Oriental Black (Oriental Ebony)

(The body standard laid down for all varieties of Oriental Shorthairs requires a body of medium size, longish, lissom and long-necked. It should not be too thin. The legs should be finely proportioned, the hindlegs being slightly longer than the front legs. The paws should be neat and oval. The tail is long, tapering to a sharp point. All the characteristics should be well-proportioned and well-balanced as regards length.

The slenderness and elegance of the body of the Oriental Shorthair is best seen in the Oriental Black (Oriental Ebony) variety (1, 2). It was named after the jet black colour of ebony wood. The combination of the jet black body colour and lissom body type is much more impressive in comparison with more sturdily built blacks of other breeds. This variety should not only conform to the requirement of a black glossy coat, but it should also show a black muzzle and foot pads (3). The full colour appears relatively late, only when the cat is about two to three years old.

Apart from the elegance, which can stand comparison with the Siamese, Oriental Shorthairs are reputed to be extremely active, being great climbers. On the other hand, they are said to be more affectionate and playful and even more intelligent. When in season, their voices are more melodious and less penetrating than those of the Siamese.

3

Although there is no evident shading or varying colour intensity in the coat of an Oriental Black, it always carries the genes determining points colours. Therefore, a Siamese-type kitten may crop up in the litter of an Oriental Black, be it a Blue Point, Chocolate Point, Lilac Point and/or an Oriental Blue or Havana, in addition to an Oriental Lilac. As with the Oriental White, the Oriental Black female can also be mated to the Siamese male so as to improve the head type (for genes determining black colour are dominant). If so, the only risk breeders take is a deterioration of the green eye colour.

Oriental Lilac (Lavender)

The colours of all varieties of Oriental Shorthairs are equivalent to those of the other Shorthairs, for example British and European, yet a distinct difference is seen in the head type. The head of the Oriental Shorthair is long and wedge-shaped. The face should narrow in straight lines to a fine muzzle. The chin is well-developed, yet not too strong. The forehead and nose should be straight. The eyes should be set well apart (the distance between them should be an eye's width), slanting towards the nose (hence the name 'Oriental' Shorthair). As with other cats, a squint is regarded as undesirable, disqualifying the specimen from further breeding. The ears of Oriental Shorthairs are large, and set well apart at the base.

The Oriental Lilac (1, 2) is identical in colour to the Lilac Point Siamese. The soft and glossy coat should be a light grey colour with a fine pinkish tone. A bluish tone is not desirable, in spite of being found rather frequently. The muzzle and paw pads are a lavender pink, showing a shade similar to that of the ground colour of the coat. The eyes are usually apple green (3). Oriental Lilacs were given recognition in 1972.

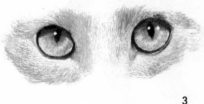

3

Oriental Shorthairs usually show a paler shading on the chin and chest. The shading is acceptable in judging, provided it is restricted to light beige patches. Larger amounts of white hair, however, disqualify an animal from breeding. They appear on other parts of the body, namely on the legs and around the eyes, where they form a pair of spectacles. The large patches are caused by the presence of the gene for white spotting. Unless white patches are prescribed by the standard, they are considered to be definite faults.

2

1

Oriental Tabby

Patterned (Tabby) Orientals constitute nearly three-quarters of the overall number of Oriental Shorthairs recognized by standards. As already mentioned with British Shorthairs, Oriental Shorthairs are of three tabby pattern types — mackerel, blotched and spotted. According to the dominant colour, Oriental Shorthairs are divided into the following subgroups — black, blue, chocolate, lilac, red, cream and silver (which is further divided into four colour combinations). Each variant listed is recognized as a separate variety of Oriental Shorthairs. Consequently, there is an overall number of 30 tabby varieties. In practice, however, there are very few of them.

We have selected the Oriental Silver Mackerel Tabby (1) and the Oriental Chocolate Tabby (2) from a wide range of existing varieties. It is clearly visible that the markings are less prominent than in the more massively built British Shorthairs of the same colouring. The Oriental Tortoiseshell Tabby (3) often attracts the attention of show visitors, displaying an interesting contrast between the coat colouring and the green eye colour.

3

A hereditary loss of the agouti-factor results in another colour variety — Smoke Oriental Shorthair, with a platinum-coloured undercoat and rich green eyes (copper eyes are also widely found). Other silver varieties result from the presence of the agouti-factor. These are Chinchilla Orientals, Shaded Silver Orientals and Cameo Orientals. All the varieties mentioned have already been developed, yet they still await official recognition.

2

1

Havana (Oriental Chestnut)

The brown-coloured Havana (1) is the oldest-known colour variety of Oriental Shorthair. The breed was mentioned in cat literature as early as 1888 under the name of 'self chocolate Siamese'. In 1894, a brown cat was exhibited in Britain, being described as the Swiss Mountain Cat. Today, its actual appearance is unknown, yet it might have been the ancestor of the present Havana. As late as 1950, several British breeders set about producing the present Havana of Oriental type. In 1958, it was recognized as a separate breed under the name of Chestnut Brown Foreign. In 1971, the name was changed to Havana, possibly because the cat is similar in colour to the world-renowned Cuban cigars, though it might well have been after the rabbit breed of the same name. Since the Havana had been recognized earlier than the other varieties of Oriental Shorthairs, it has become the custom not to group it with them, although it actually is an Oriental Shorthair.

The coat of the Havana should be of an even colour shade throughout, from the roots to the tips. Any shade of brown is acceptable. Breeders should ensure that the colour does not shade into the undesirable black colour. Barrings or patches as well as dark and/or light hairs are faults. When compared with the Brown Burmese, which shows a similar shade of brown, there is no darker shading of the coat on the face, ears, legs and tail. The body of the Havana is much slimmer than that of the Brown Burmese. The slanting eyes are intense green. The head (2) should be quite long, though not too elongated, with the forehead slanting backward and a distinct stop at the eyes. The muzzle and whiskers are of the same colour as the glossy coat. The Havana is the only variety which had the colour of the whiskers prescribed by former standards. The paw pads are a cinnamon pink.

Litters normally contain two to three kittens, which are born slightly paler than the shade they acquire with the moult of the kitten coat. Faint tabby stripes as well as reddish or rusty patches disappear at maturity.

The personalities of Havanas are similar to those of Siamese in many respects, except that they have slightly lower voices. Due to their more placid temperament, they make agreeable family pets, which usually become fully devoted to one person. They do not particularly like dogs. They often live to an old age; about 13 to 17 years.

Egyptian Mau

Some 30 years ago, American breeders attempted to re-establish the original type of Egyptian cat, which is said to have been a catcher of fish and vermin. Several specimens of shorthaired cats were actually taken direct from Cairo to the United States. They were claimed to have been identical to the original Egyptian spotted tabby. Later, the breed was given recognition by several North American associations. It has not yet been recognized in Great Britain or on the Continent.

It is a graceful, lissom cat of medium length. The legs are slender, the hindlegs being slightly longer than the front ones. The overall impression is that of a svelte-looking animal with fine narrow paws, oval or slightly rounded in shape. The legs should be finely striped, the stripes occasionally breaking into spots. The tail is of medium length, wide at the base, and tapering to a point. The coat is thick and short, though longer than with Siamese and Orientals to which the Egyptian Mau bears a considerable resemblance. As with Abyssinians, there are two to three bands of ticking on each hair. The back should be marked with distinct spots, preferably round and evenly distributed. The spots are smaller than those of the Spotted British Shorthair.

The head is a slightly rounded wedge; neither full cheeks nor muzzle pinch are desirable. The nose is longish and straight, the unusually fine break being seen only in profile. The fine muzzle is slate pink, rimmed with black or dark brown, and so are lips and eyes. The ears are large, slightly pointed, wide at the base and set wide apart. They are a light pink tone, nearly transparent, and furnished with fine short hair. The almond-shaped eyes are rather large, and green or golden in colour. They should be slightly slanting yet fully oriental eyes are a fault.

'Mau' is the Egyptian word for cat. So far, only three varieties of Egyptian Maus have been developed — silver (2) (black spots on a silver background); bronze (1) showing dark brown to blackish brown spots laid upon the bronze-coloured coat; and smoke, with jet black markings on a charcoal-grey background. In all cases, the colouring has not yet become fully established and therefore bronze Maus showing darker (3) or lighter shades of bronze are to be found quite frequently.

1

2

3

Index

223